THE THREE LIVES OF HELEN KELLER

Also by Richard Harrity
and Ralph G. Martin

ELEANOR ROOSEVELT: HER LIFE IN PICTURES
THE HUMAN SIDE OF FDR
MAN OF DESTINY: DE GAULLE OF FRANCE

THE
THREE LIVES
OF
HELEN KELLER

**Richard Harrity
and
Ralph G. Martin**

Doubleday & Company, Inc.
Garden City, New York
1962

I thank God for my handicaps for through them I have found myself, my work, and my God."

These are the words of Helen Keller who in over eighty gallant years of existence has lived three distinct lives, milestones in the triumph of the human spirit over affliction, utter isolation, and despair.

Stricken by a strange disease when she was almost nineteen months old that left her so that she could not hear or see, Helen Keller began a life of loneliness in the sudden silence and blackness of a strange world that cut her off from all she knew and loved. As her young mind developed, she fought furiously to free herself.

"Sometimes I stood between two people who were conversing and touched their lips," Helen Keller later recalled. "I could not understand and was vexed. I moved my lips and gesticulated frantically without result. This made me so angry at times that I kicked and screamed until I was exhausted."

Her father, Captain Arthur H. Keller, editor of a newspaper in the small Alabama town of Tuscumbia, and his wife Kate took their little daughter to hospital after hospital and specialist after specialist without receiving any help or even encouragement. It seemed that the unfortunate child was fated to live her life untutored and alone. Then one day Mrs. Keller, while reading Charles Dickens' *American Notes,* learned about a deaf and blind child, Laura Bridgman, who had been taught by Dr. Samuel Gridley Howe of the Perkins Institution in Boston to communicate with others through a manual alphabet. If one child could be saved, so could hers. But Laura Bridgman had been taught over fifty years before and Dr. Howe was dead. When, however, the Kellers brought Helen to see Alexander Graham Bell, who was deeply interested in the problems of the deaf and who had invented the telephone while seeking ways to help them "hear" through visual sound waves, he strongly recommended that Captain Keller should seek a teacher for his child at the same Perkins Institution. Dr. Bell pointed out that Laura Bridgman was still alive and still lived in Boston.

7

At the Perkins Institution, Captain Keller was told that there was but one teacher available—a twenty-one-year-old girl, Anne Sullivan, daughter of Irish immigrants, who had been half-blind herself as a child, and who had spent several years neglected in a Boston poorhouse before being admitted to the Perkins Institution to improve her sight. These were not very imposing recommendations for the difficult and delicate task of trying to establish contact with the seemingly undeveloped mind of a little girl, but Anne Sullivan lived in the same house with Laura Bridgman and was an expert at manual language. The desperate father accepted her.

Anne Sullivan arrived at the Keller homestead in Alabama early in 1887 and through patience and perseverance finally roused the first spark in the child's mind by teaching her the meaning of words attached to things and how to talk and express her thoughts with her fingers. So stirring and memorable was this first step leading from darkness into daylight that a lifetime later in London, on the day Helen Keller was seventy-five, she told a reporter: "My birthday can never mean as much to me as the arrival of Anne Sullivan on March 3, 1887. That was my soul's birthday." It was also the beginning of Helen Keller's second life.

After the first contact had been made, Anne Sullivan lovingly guided Helen Keller into leading a normal life. She took her for walks in the woods and through the countryside, describing the beauties and wonders of nature and animals, taught her to swim and ride and play like other children, and to share the joys of her devoted family. Then began the formal training that eventually made Helen Keller one of the best educated women in the world.

In time, too, Helen Keller was enabled to earn her own livelihood through lecturing and writing, and the famous of the world became her friends.

But Helen Keller's third life is the most important and the dearest to her heart—her tireless efforts over the past four decades in creating better understanding of the deaf and the blind everywhere on earth, and in raising money to help them. She has visited every state in the Union time after time, covered every continent and nearly every country during six grueling world tours, and raised vast sums to provide better care and education for those afflicted as she is. In this great and unselfish crusade she has done more for the silent and the sightless of the world than anyone who ever lived. And to this day Helen Keller still abides by this shining statement she made long ago:

"Life is an exciting business and most exciting when lived for others."

Endowed with an alert and active mind, seven-year-old Helen Keller had a great urge to know but no way to satisfy it, causing her to strike out at life with all the fury in her little body.

"I had a battle royal with Helen this morning," wrote Anne Sullivan shortly after she arrived at the Keller homestead.

8

She was referring to a scene at breakfast when she had made Helen (who had dreadful table manners, grabbing food off other people's plates and eating with her hands) use a spoon.

"Naturally the family was much disturbed and left the room," Anne Sullivan reported. "I locked the dining-room door and proceeded to eat my breakfast, though the food almost choked me. Helen was lying on the floor kicking and screaming and trying to pull my chair from under me. She kept this up for a half hour, then got up to see what I was doing. I let her see I was eating, but did not let her put her hand in the plate. She pinched me and I slapped her every time she did it. Then she went all around the table to see who was there and finding no one but me she seemed bewildered. After a few minutes, she came back to her plate and began to eat her breakfast with her fingers. I gave her a spoon which she threw on the floor. I forced her out of the chair and made her pick it up. Finally I succeeded in getting her back in her chair again, and held the spoon in her hand, compelling her to take up the food with it and put it in her mouth. In a few minutes she yielded and finished her breakfast peaceably. Then we had another tussle over folding her napkin. When she had finished, she threw it on the floor and ran toward the door. Finding it locked, she began to kick and scream all over again. It was another hour before I succeeded in getting her napkin folded. Then I let her out into the warm sunshine and went up to my room and threw myself on the bed, exhausted. I had a good cry and felt better. . . . I suppose I shall have many such battles with the little woman before she learns the only two essential things I can teach her, obedience and love."

Deciding that the best way to instruct the child was to remove her from the family circle for a while, the teacher and Helen moved into a garden house, some distance from the main house. There Anne Sullivan spent hour after hour trying to break through the barriers that separated them, tapping words endlessly into the child's hand, hoping and praying that she would understand just one. But while Helen could tap the words back correctly, they had no meaning for her. Then, on April 5, 1887, Anne Sullivan sent the following report to the Perkins Institution:

". . . This morning, while she was washing, she wanted to know the name for 'water.' When she wants to know the name of anything, she points to it and pats my hand. I spelled 'w a t e r' and thought no more about it until after breakfast. . . . We went out to the pump house, and I made Helen hold her mug under the spout while I pumped. As the cold water gushed forth, filling the mug, I spelled 'w a t e r' into Helen's free hand. The word coming so close upon the sensation of cold water rushing over her hand seemed to startle her. She dropped the mug and stood as one transfixed. A new light came over her face. She spelled 'w a t e r' several times. Then she dropped on the ground and asked for its name and pointed to the pump and the trellis, and suddenly turning round she asked for my name. I spelled 'Teacher'. . . ."

"It was as if I had come back to life after being dead. . . ." Helen Keller wrote years afterwards. "Delicious sensations rippled through me, and sweet strange things that were locked up in my heart began to sing."

With the one word "water" a miracle had been wrought—Helen Keller, deaf, dumb, blind, and lost, had been reunited with the human race, and "Teacher" became the channel through which literature, history, poetry, the Bible, and knowledge in all its glory was to flow into a thirsty mind.

After Helen Keller's awakening, her ardent nature took "joyous interest in everybody and everything" and her freed mind grew in sudden splendor. Quickly she learned Braille, reading every book her hungry hands could hold, while Anne Sullivan's fingers grew tired tapping out answers to questions inspired by the child's soaring imagination. At ten, after eleven lessons, Helen Keller uttered this memorable sentence which she repeated over and over: "I . . . am . . . not . . . dumb . . . now," and not long afterward she was able to read aloud to John Greenleaf Whittier his "In School Days." She could "hear" and understand music through the vibrations made by various instruments, and appreciate art by feeling the formation and features of a sculptured figure. By placing her fingers on the lips of a person she could tell what he was saying. She had also begun the study of languages and had had her first article published.

Even as a young girl, Helen Keller's amazing accomplishments had made her famous all over the world.

Edward Everett Hale and Oliver Wendell Holmes became her friends and marveled at the richness of her thoughts, her command of English, her zest for life, and her self-sufficiency. Phillips Brooks, the famous New England divine, instructed her in religion, and she wore off the Braille dots from page after page of her Bible, fingering her favorite passages; Alexander Graham Bell explained the mysteries of science to her and later encouraged her to write about the important issues of the day; and Mark Twain, calling her "the greatest woman since Joan of Arc," helped raise some of the money for her education.

Later, Jo Davidson, the famous sculptor, was struck by her deep belief in God and said of her, "We are all good when we are with Helen"; Alfred Einstein spoke of her "holy curiosity"; and she made even Calvin Coolidge smile.

In spite of her handicaps Helen Keller was determined to go through college and at an early age had selected the one she wanted to attend.

"When I was a little girl," she later recalled, "I visited Wellesley and surprised my friends by the announcement: 'Someday I shall go to college —but I shall go to Harvard.' When asked why I would not go to Wellesley, I replied that there were only girls there."

She was fully aware that to gain admission to college she would have to pass stiff examinations and undergo intensive preparation for them at a school for girls who could see and hear. Many of her friends strongly opposed this plan, but Helen, backed by Anne Sullivan, stubbornly stuck to her course and set out to find the right school. At the suggestion of

10

Elizabeth Cary Agassiz, President Emeritus of Radcliffe College, they called on Arthur Gilman, director of the Cambridge School for Young Ladies.

At first Mr. Gilman did not think their plan was feasible. He felt that there would be too many obstacles for Helen, but their eagerness and determination finally won him over, and in October, 1896, he admitted Helen to his school.

Mr. Gilman arranged for Anne Sullivan to accompany Helen to classes and made sure that all his teachers took extra care to understand the girl's indistinct manner of speaking. Furthermore, both he and Frau Gröte, the German teacher, learned the manual alphabet in order to communicate with Helen and take some of the strain from Anne Sullivan. Aside from these special arrangements Helen kept to the regular regimen of the school, eating and sleeping, studying and playing with the other students.

"The actual school work during the year showed little difference between the treatment of Helen and the other pupils," Mr. Gilman wrote at the time. "Miss Sullivan sat at Helen's side in the classes, interpreting to her with infinite patience the instructions of every teacher. In study hours Miss Sullivan's labors were even more arduous, for she was obliged to read everything that Helen had to learn, excepting what was prepared in Braille; she searched the lexicons and encyclopedias and gave Helen the benefit of it all."

In an article Mr. Gilman was commissioned at this time to prepare for the *Century Magazine*, he wrote:

"I could do little for Miss Keller were it not that Miss Sullivan continues her loving superintendence, and follows her with the ministrations she has so willingly rendered all these years. Thus, while the direction of Helen's intellectual work has been committed to me, I find it necessary to depend upon Miss Sullivan for certain assistance which no acquaintance less thorough and familiar with the past would be sufficient to suggest. I am day by day impressed by the magnitude of the work that we are called upon to perform for this marvelous girl, and I can only trust that I may be in some degree equal to the demand.

"Miss Sullivan and I have always before us a sense of the novelty of the work, and we feel that we cannot lay it out far in advance. We are obliged to be constantly on the alert, watching developments, and prepared to do whatever is best at the time."

Overcoming every difficulty, Helen made such strides in her studies in the first few months at the school that it was decided she would be ready to take the preliminary college entrance examinations in June, 1897. Mr. Gilman then solved the thorny question as to how Helen was to take these tests.

"At Harvard, the candidates are numbered and to those who determine the value of their work they are known by numbers only," Gilman stated in a report on her first year of college preparatory work. "It was impossible to conceal the fact that Helen's papers were written by her, because she was obliged to use the typewriter and all other candidates would use pen or pencil. Someone would be obliged to serve as eyes for Miss Keller—someone who could testify that she was the person who actually produced the written paper. Miss Sullivan naturally felt unwilling to act in this capacity. . . . It finally became plain to all that I was the proper person."

Mr. Gilman arranged with the Harvard authorities to have a separate room set aside for them so that Helen's typing would not disturb the other students, then seated beside her he tapped the questions into her hand.

The results of these examinations were most gratifying. "She was successful in every subject and took 'honors' in English and German," reported Mr. Gilman. "I think that I may say that no candidate in Harvard or Radcliffe College was graded higher than Helen in English. The result is remarkable especially when we consider that Helen has been studying on strictly college preparatory lines for one year only. She had had long and careful instruction, it is true, and she had had always the loving ministrations of Miss Sullivan. . . . No man or woman has ever in my experience got ready for these examinations in so brief a time. . . . When Helen went home, Miss Sullivan went with her, and it was hers to satisfy the busy, unintermitting demands of the intensively active brain, for, though others gladly helped, there were many matters which could be treated only by the one teacher who had awakened the activity and had followed its development from the first. Now it was a German grammar which had to be read, now a French story, and then some passage from Caesar's *Commentaries*. It looked like drudgery and drudgery it would certainly have been had not love shed its benign influence over all, lightening each step and turning hardship into pleasure."

Helen and Anne were spending the vacation period at Wrentham, Massachusetts, and immediately upon receiving her marks, Helen wrote to Mr. Gilman: "Your letter with its pleasant news was very welcome. I have thought of you often since I left Cambridge, and missed you sadly.

"I am having a delightful time, and have almost forgotten that there were any tiresome examinations. Of course, I was glad to hear that I had passed them satisfactorily. But what I consider my crown of success is the happiness and pleasure that my victory has brought to dear Teacher."

During that same summer Mr. Gilman performed another kindness to the Keller family by offering to give Helen's younger sister, Mildred, a full scholarship at the school so that the two sisters could be together.

As a result of all this, when Helen returned to school in the fall the future seemed bright indeed. Her sister whom she deeply loved was with her, and having passed nine of the sixteen hours needed for college, she began the new year's work with eagerness and confidence. Then in this seemingly serene atmosphere a drama began to develop which was to cause both Helen and her teacher great unhappiness and heartache.

After Helen's signal success in her first examinations, Anne Sullivan felt that her pupil could safely complete her preparatory course during the next two years. Mr. Gilman, however, was equally firm in the belief that Helen should spend at least three more years at his school. Anne was forced to accept this new arrangement against her better judgment and

12

began to suspect that Mr. Gilman wanted Helen to remain simply because her presence there gave his school wide publicity. From all the evidence now available, it seems that Mr. Gilman wanted even more than that— to separate Anne Sullivan from Helen and take charge of the remarkable child's education himself.

He began his campaign by curtailing Helen's studies, on the grounds that Anne was cruelly overworking her. In November, Helen was not well, and she had been having particular difficulty with her geometry. Anne decided to keep her in bed over one weekend. Gilman seized upon this as proof that the child was overtaxed and that Anne Sullivan was responsible. Using this incident as a pretext, he sent letters to Mrs. Keller, Dr. Bell, and many of Helen's benefactors in which he accused Anne of forcing the child to work beyond her capacities. To a friend, he wrote reiterating that he had always been opposed to Anne Sullivan's insistence on a two-year course of study for Helen. When his other teachers had told him that Helen was being overworked, he had protested to Anne and said he could not be responsible for Helen's health unless the three-year course was followed. Anne's answer had been, Mr. Gilman wrote, that she would remove Helen to another school. He had written to Mrs. Keller, and others, and was now awaiting word from her since no remonstrances had any effect on Anne Sullivan. He even went on to say that the pressure of work had reacted on Miss Sullivan herself, that she had lost the patience he had noted in her earlier and was often irritable and treated Helen in a way that would have caused him to dismiss any other teacher in his school.

A month later Helen Keller herself answered these charges in a moving statement which she entitled "A Terrible Extreme" and which reads in part:

". . . What I am going to write, I never fully understood until now. Mr. Gilman was evidently angry with Miss Sullivan when he heard of my slight trouble. At any rate, he insisted that she had carried it too far, and that my program must be changed as soon as possible. Miss Sullivan talked earnestly with him telling him how it all happened; but he refused to listen, and pursued his plan after his own pleasure. He wrote to some of our best friends, Mrs. Hutton, Mrs. Fuller, and others, declaring that Miss Sullivan, my true, faithful friend, was 'killing Helen with work.' He even wrote to my mother, and a long, cruel letter it was. He said I worked on Saturdays and Sundays, had no time to see the other girls, and was altogether in 'a very precarious condition.' He even went on to say that Miss Sullivan took me away from school at recess so as to prevent me from playing with the girls. . . .

"After the Thanksgiving vacation, I found my program much changed. Geometry and astronomy had been taken out, and, hardest of all, I was to have only two lessons on several of the weekdays, and not a single one after recess!

"Oh, the humiliation was harder than I could bear! It seemed as if I had been cheated out of my proper share in the school work. I knew that Miss Sullivan's judgment had been flung aside as of no value; and I knew, too, that she loved me and had taken the best care of me for nearly eleven years, and that no harm had come to me while I was with her. She had worked all these years to make my life sweet and happy. I had never overworked in my whole life, and *she* had. I remembered, with a sharp pang, how she used to suffer greatly in body, and how she had never recovered entirely from the effects of her overwork. Then, too, there were the falsehoods that Mr. Gilman had written about us. Working on Saturdays and Sundays, when all the time I had not touched a study book on Sundays, nor worked more than an hour or two on Saturdays! Miss Sullivan and I went away almost every Saturday or Sunday; and as to the other girls, I was staying at Howells House, one of the houses connected with Mr. Gilman's school, and there was no other girl beside me, except my little sister, and Mr. Gilman himself had put us there. I could not willingly have left the Hall, the other house, where I had spent such a delightful month, but for dear Miss Sullivan's sake. She seemed so nervous and tired. I thought Howells House would be the best place for her. I always saw the girls and played with them at recess, and left the school to get my lunch, because I like it best at Howells, and I wanted a short run before the bell rang, calling us back to our lessons!

"But the worst was yet to come. I went on trying to do my duty, and to think that Mr. Gilman was doing what he thought was right. But my pleasure in work was gone, and poor Miss Sullivan's situation smote me keenly.

"Then, all of a sudden, the most dreadful sorrow burst upon us which we ever had endured. On the eighth of December, I had just finished my Greek lesson, and spoke to Miss Sullivan. I touched her trembling hand, and at once saw that something terrible had happened. 'What is it, Teacher?' I cried in dismay. 'Helen,' she spelled with difficulty, 'I fear we are going to be separated!' 'What, separated? What do you mean?' I said, utterly bewildered. She said something about a letter she had received from someone, who expressed his opinion to my mother that Miss Sullivan and I should be separated. Mr. Gilman, whom I had loved and trusted, had done it all." [On that same day, December 8, 1897, Mr. Gilman had received from Helen's mother, to whom he had sent a complete charge against Anne Sullivan demanding action, a telegram which read: "You are authorized to act as Helen's guardian."]

"That very night, Mr. Gilman came in and asked for me. Oh, I do not know how I could ever have borne to see him! His very manner, pleasant and unchanged as it was, rendered it more fearful.

"A few minutes later I was bitterly telling him about that cruel letter, which seemed to doom my beloved teacher and me to ceaseless pain and sorrow. Suddenly a gentle hand touched my shoulder, and 'Don't, dear child,' said Miss Sullivan gently. Then she exchanged a few hasty words with Mr. Gilman, who wanted my little sister and me to come with him to his house for the night. He said he had received a telegram from my mother requesting him to take charge of me, and he tried to persuade me to go.

14

He said he would care for me as if I were his own daughter, and that my mother had a right to me. But, of course, I did not believe him! I could not think my mother would ever allow anything of that kind to happen. I said I would not go, and after much talking, to no purpose, he went away.

"That night my poor teacher left Howells House, and fled to our dear friend, Mrs. Fuller. That was the only resource left to her in her distress. I could not go with her, and had to stay with my little sister. Poor child, it was terrible for her too. She loved Miss Sullivan, and stood bravely by her.

"The next morning, after the saddest, weariest night, I went to the Hall. Mr. Gilman desired it, and kept talking about my finding comfort in the society of the girls. There I wrestled with my sorrow, fear, and despair all alone. Someone was with me, but she was a stranger, and my little sister was at school. My suffering was most intense: to be separated from my dear teacher, and perhaps never to see her again—the thought almost killing me. Only a true, loving heart can understand the agony I suffered when I thought of my teacher insulted, betrayed, and driven from me, and for what offense? She had done her duty faithfully, even when her poor eyes were aching so she could hardly see the lesson she was reading to me. Mr. Gilman said that he had heard the teachers say that she was cruel. She is always infinitely loving. He said, too, that his medical advisers told him my health was breaking down. I had never seen a doctor since I had been in his school; and all that term I had had no headache or any symptom which indicated overwork. Mr. Gilman said my teacher hindered me in my work. She had done her utmost to facilitate my studies; she had helped me more than they thought. One of my troubles in my work was that I had neither a Greek typewriter nor an algebra writer. But after awhile, Mr. Rogers gave me a Greek typewriter, and I got accustomed to the rest of my apparatus; and, strange to say, everything was going smoothly when Mr. Gilman cut my program.

"When I was at the Hall, Mr. Gilman came to see me for a few minutes, and told me that my father, before his death, had wished my teacher and me to be separated. He said my mother had written this in one of her letters to him and he hoped I would respect her wishes. The shock almost stunned me. But I retorted that if my dear father had understood the whole matter, and known how dearly I loved and cherished my teacher, he would never have entertained a thought of separating us.

"An hour passed, slowly, slowly on, and at last my teacher succeeded in getting to me. Mr. Gilman had kept her away from me for two hours and a half, even though he knew that I needed her sorely.

"Now our worst worry is over, and nothing could have induced me to put it down in written words if I had been the only person to suffer. I should have buried it in the depths of silence. But my teacher and I have been plunged into this misery; we have struggled together through a maze of falsehood and injustice, and we have landed together on the firm, safe stand of Right and Justice. Nevertheless, I feel that I ought to make a statement of our sorrow; so that all my friends may know the real truth, and understand that my dear, faithful teacher has never, never deserved the cruel things that Mr. Gilman has said about her. If Mr. Gilman dreamed how much I loved my teacher, I do not believe he would have dared to do the things he did. This terrible experience has made a woman of me. My childhood has slipped away with its simple, unreasoning trust in human goodness, and its dreamy unconsciousness of the evil there is in the world. I know now that men can be false and wicked, even while they seem kind and true. I have found that I cannot always put my hand in another's with a trustful spirit. Yet I know that goodness is mightier than evil, and my heart still tells me that love is the most beautiful thing in the whole world and must triumph in the end."

And love in this case did triumph, thanks to Mrs. Keller, who had once written Anne Sullivan: "I always think of Helen as partly your child. . . ." Mrs. Keller arrived at Cambridge and demanded that Helen be again placed in Anne's care.

"I really did not realize at the time what a cruel thing I was doing," explained Mrs. Keller. "Very soon the injustice of it overcame me, and I had already decided to come to Boston when Miss Sullivan's telegram 'We need you' brought me on the first train. I found Mr. Gilman had made very cruel use of the authority I had given him to distress my children and Miss Sullivan after ten years of service. I certainly never dreamed of Miss Sullivan being forced away from Helen."

Never again were they threatened with separation.

Helen and her teacher left the Cambridge School just before Christmas in 1897 and went to stay with their friends the Chamberlins in Wrentham, while Mrs. Keller took Mildred home with her. A private tutor was soon obtained for Helen, and two years later, as Anne Sullivan had predicted, the girl passed all her entrance examinations and was admitted to Radcliffe College.

With Anne Sullivan accompanying her to classes, still tapping the lectures into her hand, Helen graduated *cum laude* in competition with girls who could see and hear, in 1904. While at Radcliffe she mastered Greek, Latin, German, and French and wrote her autobiography, *The Story of My Life*, which has now been published in over fifty languages.

After graduation she and Anne Sullivan moved to a farmhouse which they had bought at Wrentham, Massachusetts. Here she continued to write. And here, some time later, Helen Keller knew the one romance of her life.

When Helen Keller was still a young girl growing into the wonder of language, Teacher spelled into her hand: "I love Helen."

And, quickly, Helen wanted to know, "What is love?"

Anne Sullivan took Helen's hand, pointed it to her own heart, and said, "It is here."

Still puzzled by an abstract idea, Helen probed deeper: "Is love the sweetness of the flowers?"

16

"No," said Teacher.

The sun was warm and bright and Helen pointed in its direction. "Is this not love?"

Teacher tried to explain: "Love," she said, "is something like the clouds that were in the sky before the sun came out. You cannot touch the clouds, you know; but you can feel the rain. You cannot touch love either, but you feel the sweetness that it pours into everything. Without love you would not be happy. . . ."

Later, when the young girl became the young woman, her oldest friend and benefactor, Alexander Graham Bell, talked to her tenderly:

"It seems to me, Helen," he said, "a day must come when love, which is more than a friendship, will knock at the door of your heart and demand to be let in."

Her answer was shy: "I do think of love sometimes," she said. "It is like a beautiful flower which I may not touch, but whose fragrance makes the garden a place of delight just the same."

And Dr. Bell answered: "Do you think that just because you cannot see or hear, you are debarred from the supreme happiness of women."

Helen protested she needed no such love—she had Teacher, her mother, her dear friends.

Dr. Bell persisted. "Life does strange things to us," he said. "You may not always have your mother, and in the nature of things, Miss Sullivan will marry, and there may be a barren stretch in your life when you will be very lonely."

It made her muse: "I can't imagine a man wanting to marry me. I should think it would seem like marrying a statue."

Then Dr. Bell said: "If a good man should desire to make you his wife, don't let anyone persuade you to forego that happiness."

He spoke from the deep warmth of his own knowledge. His own wife had been deaf since she was four years old; his own marriage was supremely happy.

Teacher Anne Sullivan did fall in love, did want to marry—the barren stretch of loneliness for Helen became a reality to be faced.

The one love of Anne Sullivan's life was John Macy, a teacher and author who helped edit Helen's first book and was later to write the highly praised *Spirit of American Literature*. For more than a year, Anne Sullivan continuously changed her mind about the marriage. Macy already had agreed to Anne Sullivan's feeling that Helen must always come first. Even so, Anne Sullivan wavered and wondered. Then one day she told Helen she would never marry, and Helen burst forth: "Oh Teacher. If you love John and let him go, I shall feel like a hideous accident."

So, finally, shortly after Helen's graduation from Radcliffe, Anne Sullivan married John Macy.

After the wedding, Dr. Bell cornered Helen and said, "I told you, Helen, she would marry. Are you going to take my advice now and build your own nest?"

More slowly now, Helen said, "It would be a severe handicap to any man to saddle upon him the dead weight of my infirmities."

Dr. Bell smiled and said, "You will change your mind some day, young woman, if the right man comes 'a-wooing.'"

[Some years later, during a lecture tour, a Chicago newspaperman, probing deeply, got her to talk about love and marriage. She admitted that she had received many proposals of marriage, but would not discuss them. But then she laughed and said, "All women should marry, if they can get men to marry them."]

She had her own concept of her ideal man.

"He doesn't have to be rich. I am paying my own passage through the world and am proud of it. And the ideal man doesn't have to be possessed of a college education. He must be one who thinks straight. Many men have obtained an education by their own efforts—for example, Mark Twain, one of my ideal men. For he was broad, humanly tender, yet strong and full of humor."

"Every marriage should have love," she added, "and both man and woman should never lose sight of the happiness of their children."

Suddenly these words picked up fresh meaning for her; suddenly love came to Helen Keller.

Years later, Helen quietly discussed this love in her book *Midstream,* but she never mentioned the man's name, never described him.

Helen met him when Polly Thomson, who was then her secretary, had gone home to Scotland on vacation. He was hired temporarily to accompany Helen while she was on a lecture tour. He quickly learned the manual alphabet, and Helen said, "The young man was very much in earnest and eager to have people get my message." He returned to Wrentham with Helen and Anne in the autumn of 1916.

They had been home only a short time when Mrs. Macy became ill with pleurisy complicated by extreme fatigue, and a doctor told her she must spend the winter at Lake Placid.

"That meant that our home would be broken up. I could not work, I could not think calmly," wrote Helen of this period. "For the first time in my life it seemed folly to be alive. I had often been asked what I should do if anything happened to my teacher. I was now asking myself the same question. I saw more clearly than ever before how inseparably our lives were bound together. How lonely and bleak the world would be without her. What could I do? I could not imagine myself going on with my work alone. . . . Such was the background of the adventure I shall relate.

"I was sitting alone in my study one evening," she continued, "utterly despondent. The young man, who was still acting as my secretary in the absence of Miss Thomson, came in and sat down beside me. For a long time he held my hand in silence, then he began talking to me tenderly. I was surprised that he cared so much about me. There was sweet comfort in his loving words. I listened all atremble. He was full of plans for my

18

happiness. He said if I would marry him, he would always be near to help me in the difficulties of life. He would be there to read to me, look up material for my books, and do as much as he could of the work my teacher had done for me.

"His love was a bright sun that shone upon my helplessness and isolation. The sweetness of being loved enchanted me, and I yielded to an imperious longing to be part of a man's life. For a brief space I danced in and out of the gates of Heaven, wrapped up in a web of bright imaginings. Naturally I wanted to tell my mother and my teacher about the wonderful thing that had happened to me; but the young man said, 'Better wait a bit. We must tell them together. We must try to realize what their feelings will be. Certainly they will disapprove at first. Your mother does not like me, but I shall win her approval by my devotion to you. Let us keep our love secret a little while. Your teacher is too ill to be excited just now and we must tell her first.' I had happy hours with him. We walked in the autumn splendor of the woods, and he read to me a great deal. But the secrecy which circumstances appeared to impose upon us made me suffer. The thought of not sharing my happiness with my mother and her who had been all things to me for thirty years seemed abject, and little by little it destroyed the joy of being loved.

"As we parted one night, I told him I had made up my mind definitely to tell my teacher everything the next morning."

But the next morning Helen Keller's mother came into her room in great distress with the morning newspapers. "What have you been doing with that creature?" she asked Helen. "The papers are full of a dreadful story about you and him. What does it mean? Tell me!"

"I sensed such hostility toward my lover in her manner and words," wrote Helen, "that in a panic I pretended not to know what she was talking about."

"Are you engaged to him?" her mother wanted to know. "Did you apply for a marriage license?"

"Terribly frightened and anxious to shield my lover," wrote Helen, "I denied everything. I even lied to Mrs. Macy, fearing the consequences that would result from the revelation coming to her in this shocking way. My mother ordered the young man out of the house that very day. She would not even let him speak to me, but he wrote me a note in Braille telling me where he would be and begging me to keep him informed."

Reporters called Mrs. Macy for her comment, and she said there was no truth in the assertion that Miss Keller was to be married. Soon afterward a headline stated that Mrs. Macy had left her pupil and was going alone to Lake Placid. The next news came immediately from the law offices of Raymond, Gordon and Waitman in the National Shawmut Bank Building, where Helen Keller and her mother conferred with Robert L. Raymond, and a statement was promptly released to the press denying the romance and intended marriage and insisting that Mrs. Macy's trip was on doctor's orders.

"I kept on denying that I knew anything about the story in the papers until Mrs. Macy went to Lake Placid with Miss Thomson, who had returned from Scotland," Helen wrote later, "and my mother took me home" [to Alabama].

"In time she found out how I had deceived her and everyone else. The memory of her sorrow burns me to the soul. She begged me not to write Mrs. Macy anything about it until we knew that she was stronger. 'The shock would kill her, I am sure,' she said. It was months later when my teacher learned the truth.

"I cannot account for my behavior," Helen Keller afterward noted. "As I look back and try to understand, I am completely bewildered. I seem to have acted exactly opposite to my nature. It can be explained only in the old way—that love makes us blind and leaves the mind confused and deprives it of the use of judgment.

"I corresponded with the young man for several months, but my love dream was shattered. It had flowered under an inauspicious star. The unhappiness I had caused my dear ones produced a state of mind unfavorable to the continuance of my relations with the young man. The love which had come unseen and unexpected departed with tempest on its wings.

"As time went on, the young man and I became involved in a net of falsehood and misunderstanding.

"I am sure that if Mrs. Macy had been there, she would have understood and sympathized with us both. The most cruel sorrows in life are not its losses, but its frustrations and betrayals.

"The brief love will remain in my life, a little island of joy surrounded by dark waters. I am glad that I have had the experience of being loved and desired. The fault was not in the loving, but in the circumstances."

She continued on her own course unafraid, writing other books, lecturing all over America in halls and tents, and even appearing in vaudeville to make ends meet.

But greater than her worry over finances was her concern in finding her true niche in life. There had been signposts pointing to the mission she felt she was meant to fulfill. When she was twelve, she had written letters, given parties, and campaigned to raise money to help a little blind boy, Tommy Stringer.

From this time onward she never ceased to work for the blind, making speeches, writing letters and articles, serving on commissions and committees, pleading with legislatures; but it was not until the American Foundation for the Blind was established in 1921 that she came upon the great organization which was to help her fulfill what she was destined to do—to help the blind all over the world as she herself had been helped. And so successful has she been in this, her life work, that these words of George Bernard Shaw, whom she admired, might have been written by Helen Keller herself:

"This is the true joy of life, being used for a purpose recognized by yourself as a mighty one."

20

Starting in 1921 and for the next three years Helen Keller gave three hundred lectures all over America to raise money. She wrote thousands of letters to likely contributors and thousands more to blind correspondents everywhere, prepared magazine articles telling readers how they could help less fortunate people, and trod the corridors of Congress for hours on end, lobbying for bills that would aid the sightless.

In the past forty years, Helen Keller has been received by seven presidents, visited almost all the governors of all the states, and traveled over the world six times in behalf of her great and humane cause. In Japan in 1937 on her initial world tour, she worked eighteen hours a day preparing and delivering speeches which enabled her to raise forty million yen for the blind of that country. And everywhere she has gone since, from India to Australia, from Egypt to Siam and all way stations in between, hospitals and schools for the blind have been built in her wake.

Both during and after World War II, Helen Keller made a continuous round of visits to military hospitals throughout the United States to offer help and encouragement to blinded soldiers. Thanks to her years of travel in her own country she could always establish an immediate bond with a sightless boy by talking about his home town whether it was Aberdeen, Washington, or Zenith, Ohio. She even danced with blind soldiers and sailors to show them that the ordinary pleasures of life were still within their reach.

And she preached and practiced her own favorite precepts: "Never bend your head. Always hold it high. Look the world straight in the face. Never think of your limitations. Trust in your fellow men. It's as simple as that."

"Often it was not verbal encouragement that was asked of me," she recalled after a visit to the wounded, "but a kiss or the laying of my hand on a weary hand. This always made me feel as if I were partaking of a sacrament."

Once when she bent down and kissed a blinded soldier, he said, "My, I have not had a kiss like that in years. My mother used to kiss me that way."

She also kept up with her enormous correspondence, urging contributions, answering appeals, and giving advice such as she sent to the parents of a four-year-old boy who had been blinded in both eyes: "I beg you to soften your grief by looking at his handicaps hopefully. Out of the fullness of my experience I can assure you he has a good fighting chance. You can help him win an education just like any other child. Guided by the understanding and the faith of those who study the blind and their problems he can gain knowledge and grow up strong and able to find joy in living."

In addition to her never-ending struggles to overcome her own difficulties, Helen Keller has known pain and sorrow in her triumphant march through life. Anne Sullivan Macy, the beloved teacher, who rescued her from the twin solitudes that had once engulfed her and who scarcely ever left her side, died in 1936. Helen Keller began writing a book in tribute to "Teacher" but when she was in Greece in 1946 on a campaign for the blind, her home in Connecticut burned to the ground, destroying all her possessions including the manuscript which was then over two-thirds finished. She started all over again, however, and the book was finally published in 1955 with this touching title page:

Teacher
Anne Sullivan Macy
A Tribute
By the foster child of her mind
Helen Keller

The second great blow came in 1959 when Polly Thomson—Anne Sullivan's successor and Helen's close friend and companion, who had once said of her: "After forty-one years never a day goes by that I am not amazed by her"—passed away.

"I have often thought it would be a blessing if each human being were stricken blind and deaf for a few days at a time during his early adult life," Helen Keller wrote. "Darkness would make him more appreciative of sight, silence would teach him the joys of sound."

Helen once eagerly asked a friend who had just taken a long walk through the woods what she had seen, and was amazed by the friend's reply: "Nothing in particular."

Having learned to "behold" the beauties of nature through her sense of smell and touch and to "hear" the lovely sounds of life in the vibrations caught by her sensitive finger tips, she could not imagine how anyone blessed with sight and hearing could walk through the woods for an hour and not be struck with wonder at every step.

"I who cannot see find hundreds of things to interest me through mere touch," she observed. "I feel the delicate symmetry of a leaf. I pass my hands lovingly about the smooth skin of a silver birch, or the rough shaggy bark of a pine. In spring I touch the branches of trees hopefully in search of a bud, the first sign of awakening nature after her winter's sleep. Occasionally, if I am very fortunate, I place my hand gently on a small tree and feel the happy quiver of a bird in full song."

Often her heart has hungered to hear and see the loveliness she has only felt and which her rich imagination has given form. This longing once caused her to imagine the things she would most want to see if she were granted the gift of sight for just three short days.

On the first of her three days of freedom from darkness she would assemble all her friends and "Look long into their faces. I should let my eyes rest, too, on the face of a baby so that I could catch a vision of the eager, innocent beauty which precedes the individual's consciousness of the conflicts which life develops . . . and I should like to look into the loyal, trusting eyes of my dogs, the little Scottie and the stalwart great Dane."

She would also want to look at the many books which have brightened

22

the blackness in which she has always lived, and go for a stroll along a leafy lane, savoring to the utmost the splendors of nature that those who can see so often take for granted. And she would "Pray for the glory of the sunset. That night I think I should not be able to sleep."

On her second day of seeing, she would begin by marveling at that miracle which daily transforms darkness into daylight and which Homer described as "rosy-fingered dawn." Then she would visit museums to study man's slow growth over the centuries as revealed by ancient implements, costumes, and artifacts. She would go to art museums and gaze with awe at the stone images of pagan deities, friezes, bas-reliefs, and sculptured figures that she had taught herself to know and appreciate simply through the sense of touch.

"So, on this, my second day," she dreamed, "I should try to probe into the soul of man through his art."

In the evening, Helen Keller, who treasures Shakespeare only next to the Bible, would go to the theater. "How I should like to see the fascinating figure of Hamlet or the gusty Falstaff amid colorful Elizabethan trapping."

Or—since the principal way she has been able to grasp the grace of rhythmic body movement is by tracing with her fingers the dancing figures in a frieze or sculptured grouping—she would attend a performance of the ballet, filled with movement, color, and magic.

She would begin the third and last day by watching the sunrise again; then she would visit a great city to see how people live and work. She would go to the poor sections, saunter through elegant streets, and look lovingly at children playing games in a park bright with color. She would study the expressions on the faces of people passing by her and attempt in this way to understand them and their way of life. From the expressions in their eyes she would share their joys and sorrows. In short, on this third day she would be a part of normal life in the fullest sense.

"I stroll down Fifth Avenue. I throw my eyes out of focus, so that I see no particular object but only a seething kaleidoscope of color. I am certain that the colors of the women's dresses moving in a throng must be a gorgeous spectacle of which I should never tire. But perhaps if I had sight I should be like most other women—too interested in styles to give much attention to the splendor of color in the mass."

On this final night before her return to darkness, she would go once more to the theater to witness a comedy and by observing the audience as well as the actors learn how laughter lightens so many of life's burdens.

After listing these precious things she would like to see above all else, if given the use of her eyes for a period of three days, Helen Keller concluded with this touching advice:

"I who am blind can give one hint to those who see: use your eyes as if tomorrow you would be stricken blind. And the same method can be applied to the other senses.

"Hear the music of voices, the song of a bird, the mighty strains of an orchestra as if you would be stricken deaf tomorrow. Touch each object as if tomorrow your tactile sense would fail. Smell the perfume of flowers, taste with relish each morsel as if tomorrow you could never smell and taste again. Make the most of every sense, glory in all the facets of pleasure and beauty which the world reveals to you through the several means of contact which nature provides. But of all the senses, I am sure that sight must be far and away the most delightful."

Made of the strong and shining stuff that the Lord saves for his saints, Helen Keller continues in her eighties to help others help themselves, embodying in her own being and in her amazing career that positive attitude toward life and living which she has expressed:

"When one door of happiness closes, another opens; but often we look so long at the closed door that we do not see the one which has been opened for us."

Just opposite Andrew Jackson's old house in Tuscumbia, Alabama, this fair-sized house was built of Georgia pine, covered with English ivy, and appropriately called "Ivy Green." It was on a plantation originally settled by the Caspar Keller family who came here from Switzerland by way of Maryland. One of the Keller ancestors was a daughter of a Lafayette aide and a granddaughter of a colonial governor of Georgia; the Keller cousins included the Commander-in-Chief of the Confederate Army, Robert E. Lee.

An earlier ancestor in Switzerland was the first teacher of the deaf in Zurich, and wrote a book on the subject.

C aptain Arthur H. Keller was a man of many prides: he had served ably in the Confederate Army; published the local newspaper, the *North Alabamian;* was appointed Marshal of North Alabama by President Cleveland; was noted for his fine dogs and his love of the hunt; and raised the finest strawberries and watermelons in the county.

Kate Adams, twenty years younger than the Captain, was his second wife. His first died, leaving him two grown sons. Kate Adams' family went from Massachusetts to Arkansas to Tennessee. It included both a brigadier general in the Confederate Army and Edward Everett, who spoke on the same platform with President Lincoln at Gettysburg.

Mrs. Keller watched over the pigs, turkeys, chickens, and sheep, and had a county reputation for curing hams. But her special love was an old-fashioned garden that became a paradise for her three children yet to be born, two daughters and a son.

H elen was born on June 27, 1880 in the little house adjacent to "Ivy Green"—a large, square room with an adjoining room for a servant. Mrs. Keller wanted the child called "Helen Everett," after her mother, but the forgetful father, hurrying to church, gave the child his wife's maiden name, "Helen Adams."

Helen was a delightful, bright, blue-eyed baby, imitating everybody's words and gestures like a born mimic. At six months, she amazed listeners by clearly repeating, "tea, tea, tea," and saying "How d'ye." But her favorite word was "wah-wah" for water.

T he beginning of my life was very simple," Helen wrote when she was twelve years old, "and very much like the beginning of every other little life."

She walked the day she was a year old.

She raced up to her father every evening for a kiss as he asked, "What has my little woman been doing today?"

She played games with her mother, hiding behind the huge hedge of boxwood.

"And what wonderful eyes you had," her mother later told her. "You were picking up needles and buttons which nobody could find."

Then the simple beginning quickly clouded. On a cold February day, a high fever came suddenly, mysteriously, and the doctor diagnosed it as a congestion of the stomach and brain. She was then almost nineteen months old. She was not expected to live.

As quickly as the illness came, it went. Thankfully bathing her baby the day after the crisis had passed, Mrs. Keller suddenly noted that the child's lids did not close when she passed her hand over them. And when the mother screamed, Helen never heard it.

She would never hear, never see, anything again.

"I was too young to realize what had happened," said Helen afterward. "When I awoke and found that all was dark and still, I suppose I thought it was night and I must had wondered why day was so long in coming. Gradually, however, I got used to the silence and darkness that surrounded me, and forgot that it ever had been day. Soon even my childish voice was stilled because I had ceased to hear any sound."

If any dim memory stayed perhaps it was the glimpse of "broad green fields, a luminous sky, trees and flowers."

Doctors all gave Mrs. Keller a hopeless verdict, but she kept seeking. She took Helen, then six years old, to a Baltimore oculist named Chisholm. On the train, a restless Helen strung together some shells, clung to the conductor's coattails while he punched tickets, and complained to her mother that her homemade doll had no eyes—and her mother sewed in button eyes.

Chisholm offered hope for Helen's care, not cure. He suggested they see Alexander Graham Bell. Dr. Bell was a giant of a man with a giant mind. His interest in deafness was highly personal—both his mother and wife were deaf, his wife since she was four. Bell's father had invented a system of Visible Speech, an advance in the teaching of phonetics that contributed to George Bernard Shaw's interest in the subject, as attested in the Preface to *Pygmalion*. Bell himself had invented the telephone only as a sort of by-product of a system to help his deaf pupils "see" sounds they could not hear. Bell also had organized the Volta Bureau for the deaf in Washington, D.C., promoting the oral method of instruction instead of the sign language.

Dr. Bell held Helen on his knee, let her examine his watch. "He made it strike for me," she afterward wrote. "He understood my signs and I knew it and I loved him at once."

It was Dr. Bell who suggested to Mrs. Keller that she write to Michael Anagnos, head of the Perkins Institution in Boston, about the possibility of getting a teacher for Helen. That was the summer of 1886.

Mrs. Keller had heard of Perkins Institution long before. She had read Charles Dickens' description of this school for the blind in his *American Notes:* "[It] stands a mile or two without the town, a cheerful, healthy spot; and is an airy, spacious, handsome edifice. It is built upon a height, commanding a harbor."

Dickens also wrote about Dr. Samuel Gridley Howe, fifty years before at Perkins, who had opened the closed mind of a deaf and blind child named Laura Bridgman. She had opened Howe's mind, too—previously he had considered the blind inferior to other persons in mental power and ability.

Dr. Howe was a Bostonian. After receiving his M.D. from Harvard in 1824, he went to Greece, where for six years he fought against the Turk for Greek independence and came to see his life as one of service to suffering people. For the blind, following his return to Boston, he opened a school—later to become the Perkins Institution—and set up a press for books in Braille at a time when few such books were to be had. His publications, in "Howe" type, included a geography he wrote especially for the blind and the first atlas with raised maps.

At Perkins, he even walked blindfolded through the corridors so that he could make himself increasingly aware of their obstacles.

Working with Howe, and later succeeding him as head of Perkins, was his son-in-law, Michael Anagnos, a Greek patriot born in Epirus, then under the Turk and now part of Albania.

I sometimes try to realize what my life might have been if Dr. Samuel Gridley Howe had not had the imagination to realize that the immortal spirit of Laura Bridgman had not died when her physical senses were sealed up," wrote Helen Keller.

Like Helen, Laura Bridgman had lost her sight and hearing while a child (she was two years old). Like Helen, she had blue eyes and light brown hair. Like Helen, she had been restless, willful. But there the resemblance ended.

Howe taught Laura by using raised letters on cards, repeating them until she finally realized the meaning that went with each raised word.

Helen later met Laura and described her: "To me, she seemed like a statue I had once felt in a garden. She was so motionless and her hands were so cool, like flowers that had grown in shady places."

Nobody knew better than Helen that this cool, quiet woman who made beautiful lace, spoke a few words, seldom left her room, and never left the school—that this woman had "bridged the chasm between mankind and me."

Helen described herself as "a phantom living in a no-world."

"But all was not lost," she said. "After all, sight and hearing are but two of the most beautiful blessings which God has given me. The most precious, the most wonderful of His gifts was still mine. My mind remained clear and active, 'though fled for'er the light.' "

Her mother's brother, who thought differently, told Mrs. Keller, "You really ought to put that child away, Kate. She is mentally defective, and it is not pleasant to see her about."

It was true that the child often screamed with frustration, pounding the floor because nobody understood her. Some things she could communicate: for bread and butter, she imitated the bread-cutting and butter-spreading; for ice cream, she imitated the working of a freezer, and pretended to shiver with cold.

It was a jealous child who on the arrival of a baby sister, Mildred, overturned the cradle. It was a fun-loving child who cut off a playmate's curls. It was a curious child who poured oil on her own head, covered her face with powder and a lace veil, tied a huge bustle around her waist. It was a blind child who held her wet apron to dry in front of the fire and screamed when it caught flame.

It was a deaf child, a mute child, but it was not a *dumb* child.

Anne Mansfield Sullivan had a childhood of horror. Her parents were potato-famine refugees from Limerick, Ireland, and they never could pull out of their poverty. A frustrated father gave her drunken beatings and, when his wife died, sent ten-year-old Anne and her younger brother Jimmie to a Massachusetts poorhouse where the demented mixed with the diseased.

Her brother died there, and Anne was almost blind when she was brought to Perkins four years later, a friendless girl who couldn't even spell her own name.

Some operations partly restored Anne's sight and Laura Bridgman taught her the manual alphabet—a method of spelling words with fingers, a system originally brought to France from Spain where it was supposedly invented by some Trappist monks under the vow of silence.

Anne graduated as the class valedictorian, saying, "And now we are going out into the busy world to take our share of life's burdens, and do our share of life's burdens, and do our little to make the world better, wiser, and happier." But her own future depressed her. "Here I was, twenty years old," she said, "and I realized that I didn't know a single subject thoroughly. I could not possibly teach and I had no urge to teach. I knew better than I had six years ago how abysmal my ignorance was."

Michael Anagnos disagreed. When Captain Keller asked for a teacher, Anagnos offered the job to Anne Sullivan.

She accepted with considerable question. Quickly she studied the complete records of Howe's training of Laura Bridgman. Laura herself warned Anne not to spoil Helen by letting her become disobedient. The blind girls at Perkins bought a doll as a gift for Helen, and Laura made the clothes. Then came a long train ride to Tuscumbia, and her first question, "Where is Helen?"

Many years later, Helen described the day of Anne Sullivan's arrival, March 3, 1887, as "my soul's birthday."

But she did not feel it then.

"I stood on the porch, dumb, expectant," Helen wrote later. "I guessed vaguely from my mother's signs and from the hurrying to and fro in the house that something unusual was about to happen, so I went to the door and waited on the steps."

As she stood there, her brown hair uncombed, her black shoes tied with white strings, her dress dirty, looking something like a small savage—Anne Sullivan tried to kiss her. Helen pushed her away, then rushed at her with such force that she almost knocked her down, grabbed her bag, unsuccessfully tried to open it, motioned furiously for the key and almost went into a tantrum when she didn't get it.

The situation soon worsened. Helen locked Anne in her room, hid the key, forcing her father to get a ladder so Anne could climb out the window. And Helen's table manners were appalling.

Anne Sullivan finally persuaded Captain Keller to let her take Helen alone for two weeks to a small adjacent house. Once there, Helen kicked and screamed herself into a stupor, and then came the terrific tussle at bedtime.

"The struggle lasted for nearly two hours," said Miss Sullivan. "I never saw such strength and endurance in a child. But, fortunately for us both, I am a little stronger, and quite as obstinate when I set out."

Next morning Helen was docile, but obviously homesick, going often to the door, touching her cheek, which was her sign for her mother, and shaking her head sadly. "She played with her dolls more than usual," said Miss Sullivan, "and would have nothing to do with me."

Two weeks later: "the wild Helen has become gentle, learned to crochet, learned to spell words, but still has no idea that everything has a name."

Helen even tried to teach her dog how to spell "d-o-l-l."

But when Anne Sullivan persisted in trying to associate in Helen's mind the word "d-o-l-l" and the doll in her hand, the bewildered Helen smashed the doll to pieces. Miss Sullivan later brought her to the pump, let the water run onto her hands, spelling the word "w-a-t-e-r" again and again until the light came, "the key to my kingdom," as Helen later put it. Soon afterward, Helen went back to the broken pieces of her doll, picked them up, tried vainly to put them together, and cried.

Before the incident at the water pump, Anne Sullivan had written Michael Anagnos that Helen "accepted everything I did for her as a matter of course, and refused to be caressed." But, now, with the learning of nouns, adjectives, and verbs, came love. And with love came laughter.

Helen had not laughed since she became deaf. But one day Anne Sullivan came into her room laughing gleefully, put Helen's hand on her face and spelled "laugh," and then gently tickled Helen until she, too, was laughing, again and again, until the joy was bursting, radiant. Together they jumped, skipped, tumbled, hopped.

A generation before, Dr. Samuel Gridley Howe had said, "A teacher cannot be a child."

Anne Mansfield Sullivan was otherwise convinced—a teacher *must* be a child.

Helen and Anne went for long walks, chased butterflies, sometimes caught one. "Then we sit under a tree and talk about it," said Miss Sullivan. In a letter to Anagnos, she complained, "We are bothered a great deal by people who . . . tell us that Helen is overdoing, that her mind is too active (these very people thought she had no mind at all a few months ago!) . . . and they suggest many impossible and absurd remedies. But so far, nobody seems to have thought of chloroforming her, which is, I think, the only effective way of stopping the natural exercise of her faculties."

...about every-
thing that happened on the
way home, and I do not know
when she would finish the letter
if I had not told her to say
good-by. I have not corrected
or changed the letter in any
way. She was the acknowledged
belle of Huntsville while
we stayed. Old and young
could not fail to be interested
by the bright little lady.
Never did a teacher have more
reason to be proud of a pupil.
A sweeter or brighter child it
would be impossible to find.

Tuscumbia, Alabama,
August 28, 1887

Mr. Anagnos,
    My dear Friend,
              The list of words
you were so kind to send me,
have been a great help to me,
and afforded Helen much
benefit and pleasure. Please
do not think, because you
have not heard from me before,
your kindness was unappre-
ciated. If you could have
seen Helen's joy as her fingers
discovered each familiar
name or object, you would
have been made very happy.

Toward the bottom of the second page in this letter to Anagnos, Anne Sullivan wrote, "Never did a teacher have more reason to be proud of a pupil. A sweeter or brighter child would be impossible to find."

To another friend, she added: "I want to say something which is for your ears alone. Something within me tells me I shall succeed beyond my dreams. Were it not for some circumstances that make such an idea highly improbable, even absurd, I should think Helen's education would surpass in interest and wonder Dr. Howe's achievement. I know that she has remarkable powers, and I believe that I shall be able to develop and mold them. I cannot tell how I know these things. I had no idea a short time ago how to go to work; I was feeling about in the dark, but somehow I know now, and I know that I know. I cannot explain it; but when difficulties arise, I am not perplexed or doubtful. I know how to meet them; I seem to divine Helen's peculiar needs. It is wonderful. . . .

"I shall write freely to you and tell you everything, on one condition. It is this: you must promise never to show my letters to anyone. My beautiful Helen shall not be transformed into a prodigy if I can help it."

Miss Annie, I thank God every day of my life for sending you to us," said Mrs. Keller.

Captain Keller simply held her hand, unable to find words.

It was Christmas, 1887, and Teacher (Helen always called her "Teacher") gave Helen a canary, showed her how to handle it gently, as she had showed her the daintiness of a string of dewdrops, the growing buds of a lily planted in her sunny window, the whirr of pigeon's wings, the quiver of soap bubbles.

Teacher taught zoology from fossils sent by a friend, arithmetic (which Helen liked least) by stringing beads, biology by feeling the gradual change in trapped tadpoles.

"I have tried from the beginning to talk naturally to Helen and to teach her to tell me only things that interest her and ask questions only for the sake of finding out what she wants to know."

She reads a good deal," Teacher wrote to Anagnos in her first full report on Helen in the fall of 1888. "She bends over her book with a look of intense interest, and as the forefinger of her left hand runs along the line, she spells out the word with the other hand; but often her motions are so rapid as to be unintelligible even to those accustomed to reading the swift and varied movements of her fingers."

Asked why she loved books so much, Helen said, "Because they tell me so much that is interesting about things I cannot see, and they are never tired or troubled like people. They tell me over and over what I want to know."

She added: "I must learn many things."

helen will write mother
letter papa did give hel-
en medicine mildred
will sit in swing
mildred will kiss
helen teacher did give
helen peach
ginger is sick in
bed george am .shunt
anna did give helen
lemonade dog did
stand up.
conductor did punch
ticket papa did give
helen drink of water
in can
carlotta did give helen
flowers anna will buy
helen pretty new hat
helen will hug and kiss
mother helen will come
home grandmother does
love helen

— suppose some wonder how we keep the lines so [t]ight," Helen wrote in another letter long afterward. "[W]e have a grooved board which we put between the [pag]es when we wish to write. The parallel grooves cor[res]pond to lines and when we have pressed the paper into [the]m by means of the blunt end of the pencil, it is very [eas]y to keep the words even. The small letters are all [ma]de in the grooves, while the long ones extend above [and] below them. We guide the pencil with the right hand, [and] carefully with the forefinger of the left hand to see [tha]t we shape and space letters correctly."

[H]er letters as a child were simpler:

[I] am very sorry that bumblebees and hornets and [bird]s and large flies and worms are eating all my father's [pre]cious grapes. They like juicy fruit to eat as well as [peo]ple, and they are hungry. They are not very wrong [to] eat too many grapes because they do not know [muc]h."

[S]he loved animals. At the circus they let her climb on [an e]lephant, pet a young lion. Told the young lion would [gro]w to be fierce, she said, "I will take the baby lions [hom]e and teach them to be mild." And, riding in the [carr]iage, she would not let the driver use the whip "be[caus]e poor horses will cry."

[H]elen was concentrating on stringing beads when [teac]her taught her the meaning of an abstract idea, by [gent]ly tapping the child's forehead and spelling "Think." "[In] a flash," said Helen afterward, "I knew that the [wor]d was the name for the process that was going on [in m]y head."

[So]on Helen said, "If I write what my soul thinks, then [it wil]l be visible and the words will be its body."

Teacher took Helen to Perkins for more organized classroom study. Helen's greatest delight was to find blind little children who spoke her finger language; her great sadness was caused by a kindly laundress who had picked up Helen's favorite doll Nancy —to whom she had fed countless mud pies —and washed her into shapelessness.

Writing to her mother, Helen said, "Clifton did not kiss me because he does not like to kiss little girls. He is shy. I am glad that Frank and Clarence and Robbie and Eddie and Charles and George are not very shy."

Michael Anagnos began a lengthy report on Helen with this poem:

No iron so hard, but rust will fret it;
No perch so high, but climbing will get it;
Nothing so lost, but seeking will find it;
No night so dark, but there is daylight
  behind it.

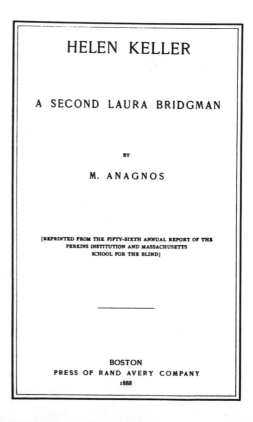

HELEN KELLER

A SECOND LAURA BRIDGMAN

BY

M. ANAGNOS

[REPRINTED FROM THE FIFTY-SIXTH ANNUAL REPORT OF THE
PERKINS INSTITUTION AND MASSACHUSETTS
SCHOOL FOR THE BLIND]

BOSTON
PRESS OF RAND AVERY COMPANY
1888

On a visit to Greece, Anagnos read to the Queen a description of a rose garden written by Helen. The Queen wept.

He also cherished this early letter of Helen's:

Mon cher Monsieur Anagnos,

I am sitting by the window and the beautiful sun is shining on me. Teacher and I came to the kindergarten yesterday. There are twenty-seven little children here and they are all blind. I am sorry because they cannot see much. Sometimes will they have very well eyes?

After a year at Perkins, Helen wrote these letters:

My precious little sister,

I go to school every day. At eight, I study arithmetic. I like that. At nine, I go to the gymnasium with the little girls and we have great fun. At ten I study about the earth in which we all live. At eleven, I talk with Teacher and at twelve I study zoology. I do not know what I shall do in the afternoon yet. . . .

When I see Lioness [Helen's dog], I will tell her many things which will surprise her greatly. I think she will laugh when I tell her she is a vertebrate, a mammal, a quadruped; and I shall be very sorry to tell her that she belongs to the order Carnivora. . .

36

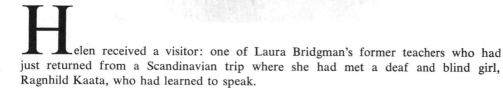

Helen received a visitor: one of Laura Bridgman's former teachers who had just returned from a Scandinavian trip where she had met a deaf and blind girl, Ragnhild Kaata, who had learned to speak.

Helen quickly spelled into Teacher's hand, "I must speak."

Anne Sullivan had been trained to teach the blind, not the deaf. Someone suggested that Helen study speech with Sarah Fuller, principal of the Horace Mann School for the Deaf, in Boston, and she went to Miss Fuller in the spring of 1890. Miss Fuller later wrote of Helen: "Her quickness of thought and her correct use of English impelled me to say, as we were going from room to room, "I believe she could learn to speak." So Helen started private lessons with Sarah Fuller.

"I began by familiarizing her with the position and condition of the various mouth parts, and with the trachea," wrote Miss Fuller. "This I did by passing her hand lightly over the lower part of my face and by putting her fingers into my mouth. I then placed my tongue in the position for the sound of "i" in it and let her find the point as it lay perfectly still and soft in the bed of the jaw, just beyond the lower front teeth, and discover that the teeth were slightly parted. After she had done this, I placed one of her forefingers upon my teeth and the other upon my throat, or trachea, at the lowest point where it may be felt, and repeated the sound "i" several times. During this time, Helen, standing in front of me in the attitude of one listening intently, gave the closest attention to every detail; and when I ceased making the sound, her fingers flew to her own mouth and throat, and after arranging her tongue and teeth, she uttered the sound "i" so nearly like that I had made, it sounded more like an echo of it."

Helen soon learned these six elements of speech: M, P, A, S, T, I. After ten lessons, she could tell Teacher, "I am not dumb now."

Teacher took over afterward with "practice, practice, practice." Watching them, one of Helen's cousins later described it: "Many times it was necessary to put her sensitive fingers in Teacher's mouth, sometimes far down into her throat, until Teacher would be nauseated, but nothing was too hard, so Helen was benefited." The biggest benefits: she could think "three times more quickly" and "my little sister will understand me now."

To Sarah Fuller, Helen wrote:

"My heart is full of joy this beautiful morning because I have learned to speak many new words, and I can make a few sentences. Last evening I went out into the yard and spoke to the moon. I said, 'O moon, come to me.' Do you think the lovely moon was glad that I could speak to her?"

Years later, Helen wrote: "Without a language of some sort, one is not a human being; without speech, one is not a complete human being. Even when the speech is not beautiful, there is a fountain of joy in uttering words. It is an emotional experience quite different from that which comes from spelled words."

Talking to a convention of teachers of the deaf when still a young girl, she said:

". . . Of course I know that it is not always easy for strangers to understand me. . . . In the meanwhile, my little sister and baby brother love to have me tell them stories in the summer evenings when I am at home; and my mother and teacher often ask me to read to them from my favorite books. I also discuss the political situation with my dear father. . . .

"I can remember the time before I learned to speak, and how I used to struggle to express my thought by means of the manual alphabet—how my thought used to beat against my finger tips like little birds striving to gain their freedom. . . ."

38

My dear Miss Grace,
The preparations for my tea in aid of the kindergarten for little blind children are nearly completed. It will be given at Mrs. Spaulding's, 99 Beacon St., next Tuesday afternoon. Will you please come? And will tell your friends and ask them to come too? I am sure they will all be interested if you tell them that I am trying to make the lives of many little helpless children bright and happy. Do come and help me. Please give my love to your mother and sisters, and believe me,
Loringly yours,
May 19th.   Helen Keller.

Teacher made Helen write her letters again and again, if necessary, until they were correct and well phrased.

The Spauldings, mentioned in this letter, were so deeply taken with Helen that they insisted on giving her financial support for many years, even giving her some stocks for savings. J. P. Spaulding promised to provide permanently for her future, but died suddenly without having made the necessary provision in his will.

The little blind boy in the picture is Tommy Stringer. One of Helen Keller's first crusades was to raise money to help provide for his education. Soon she had another fund-raising idea: "I think there are about 3000 people in Tuscumbia," she wrote, ". . . and at present there is no library of any sort in the town. That is why I thought about starting one.

"P.S. My teacher thinks it would be more businesslike to say that a list of contributors toward the building fund will be kept and published in my father's paper, the *North Alabamian.*"

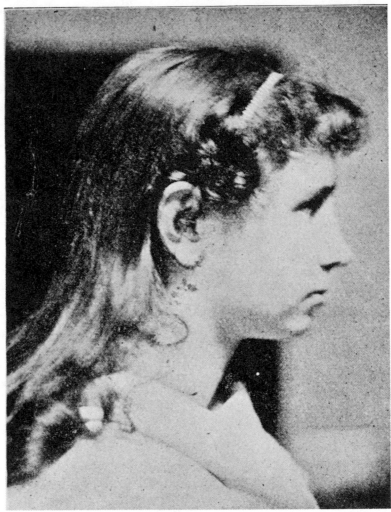

Helen was twelve years old when she spelled a story on her Braille slate to send to Mr. Anagnos on his birthday. Somebody asked if she had read it in a book and she said, "Oh, no, it is my story and I have written it for Mr. Anagnos." The family suggested the title, "The Frost King."

Mr. Anagnos was delighted with it, promptly had it published, and then came the furor. The story was strikingly similar to a story called "The Frost Fairies" by Margaret Canby in her book, *Birdie and His Friends*.

Mr. Anagnos at first sided with Helen, then set up a court of inquiry made up of four blind and four seeing persons and himself. Called in for questioning, the frightened Helen said she had no memory of the original story being read to her, that Teacher never had. The court cleared her of direct plagiarism.

"As I lay in my bed that night," said Helen, "I wept as I hope few children have wept. I felt so cold, I imagined I should die before morning. . . . I think if this sorrow had come to me when I was older, it would have broken my spirit beyond repairing."

40

THE FROST KING.

BY HELEN A. KELLER.

[*Copied from the original manuscript in the Braille writing.*]

"King Frost lives in a beautiful palace, far to the north, in the land of perpetual snow. The palace, which is magnificent beyond description, was built centuries ago, in the reign of King Glacier. At a little distance from the palace we might easily mistake it for a mountain whose peaks were mounting heavenward to receive the last kiss of the departing day. But on nearer approach we should discover our error. What we had supposed to be peaks were in reality a thousand glittering spires. Nothing could be more beautiful than the architecture of this ice-palace. The walls are curiously constructed of massive blocks of ice which terminate in cliff-like towers. The entrance to the palace is at the end of an arched recess and it is guarded night and day by twelve soldierly looking white Bears.

"But children, you must make King Frost a visit the very first opportunity you have, and see for yourselves this wonderful palace. The old king will welcome you kindly for he loves children and it is his chief delight to give them pleasure.

"You must know that King Frost, like all other kings, has great treasures of gold and precious stones; but as he is a generous old monarch he endeavors to make right use of his riches. So wherever he goes he does many wonderful works: he builds bridges over every stream, as transparent as

In the public outcry, Mark Twain made himself heard: "Oh, dear me," he wrote, "how unspeakably funny and owlishly idiotic and grotesque was that 'plagiarism' farce! As if there was much of anything in any human utterance, oral or written, except plagiarism! . . . substantially all ideas are secondhand, consciously and unconsciously drawn from a million sources."

He told of unconsciously using a dedication once used by Oliver Wendell Holmes, discovering it, telling Holmes about it, and saying, "I know where I stole it, but where did you steal it from?" And Holmes said, "I don't remember; I only know I stole it from somebody, because I have never originated anything altogether myself, or met anybody who had."

"To think of those solemn donkeys breaking a little girl's heart with their ignorant damned rubbish about plagiarism!" Mark Twain continued. "I couldn't sleep for blaspheming about it last night."

Margaret Canby, the author of "The Frost Fairies," had this feeling:

"What a wonderful, active, and retentive mind that gifted child must have! If she had remembered and written down accurately a short story, and that, soon after hearing it, it would have been a miracle, but to have heard the story once three years ago [when, as was finally determined a friend may have read it to her], and then to have been able to reproduce it so vividly, even adding some touches of her own in perfect keeping with the rest, which really improve the original, is something that very few girls of riper age with every advantage of sight and hearing and even greater talents of composition could have done so well. . . .

"Please give her my warm love and tell her not to feel troubled about it anymore. . . ."

For a long time afterward, when an idea flashed in conversation, Helen spelled to Teacher, "I do not think it is mine."

"The Frost Fairies" and "The Frost King" are given in full, as the differences are as important as the resemblances.

THE FROST FAIRIES.

BY MARGARET T. CANBY.

[*From "Birdie and his Fairy Friends."*]

"King Frost, or Jack Frost as he is sometimes called, lives in a cold country, far to the North; but every year he takes a journey over the world, in a car of golden clouds drawn by a strong and rapid steed called 'North Wind;' wherever he goes, he does many wonderful things: he builds bridges over every stream, clear as glass in appearance, but often strong as iron; he puts the flowers and plants to sleep, by one touch of his hand, and they all bow down, and sink into the warm earth, until spring returns; then, lest we should grieve for the flowers, he places at our windows lovely wreaths and sprays of his white northern flowers, or delicate little forests of fairy pine-trees, pure white, and very beautiful. But his most wonderful work is the painting of the trees,

HELEN KELLER
And Her Little Sister Mildred

Helen maintained a closeness with her sister Mildred and the relationship deepened with their father's death. "He died last Saturday at my home in Tuscumbia," Helen wrote a friend, "and I was not there. My own loving father! Oh, dear friend, how shall I ever bear it. . . ."

She gave her father great pleasure in his last days listening to his famous stories as he clumsily spelled them into her hand, and then repeating them to the rest of the family. He always brought her the first and best of his prize berries. "I remember his caressing touch as he led me from tree to tree, from vine to vine. . . ."

42

Her dear friend, Alexander Graham Bell, took Helen and her mother and Teacher to visit the World's Fair in Buffalo. They let her touch everything at the Fair from a Viking ship to a real camel.

She gave this description of nearby Niagara Falls:

"I could hardly realize that it was water that I felt rushing and plunging with impetuous fury at my feet. It seemed as if it were some living thing rushing into some terrible fate. One feels helpless and overwhelmed in the presence of such a vast force. I suppose you feel so, too, when you gaze up to the stars in the stillness of the night, do you not?"

When Mark Twain heard this vivid description, he said quietly to a friend, "I thank God she cannot see."

43

She was growing in giant strides. During a family discussion of the tariff question, Helen wanted to know about it, and Teacher spelled to her, "No, you cannot understand it yet." Helen was silent, then suddenly said, "How do you know that I cannot understand! I have a good mind! You must remember, dear Teacher, that Greek parents were very particular with their children, and they used to let them listen to wise words, and I think they understood some of them."

Another time she said, "I think it is right for men to fight against wrongs and tyrants."

[In her supersensitive way, Helen not only could recognize friends as quickly as she touched their hands or clothing, but she seemed to sense the state of mind of those around her.]

Teacher told her: "Oh, how wonderful it would be if you can accomplish complete independence, as the thirteen colonies did." Then she added, "But, remember, no matter what happens, that the real independence you can attain is in your spirit and mind."

Helen answered, "I can read, and I will devour every book I can lay my hands on."

"That is a splendid way to be independent, but it is not enough. If you grow up a bookworm, what use will you be in the world?"

Teacher kept hard at her. If she was not reading and seemed to be idling, Teacher good-naturedly would say, "For shame, you have those books full of choice words and interesting thoughts and here you sit like a calf with not a spark of expression on your face."

"Wal, now, you better just find out for yourself," exclaimed Cousin Cynthia, drawing a package from under her shawl. "You better just look at these 'ere almanacs before you go givin' on 'em away again to be burnt up—there they are just as you give 'em to me!"

The old woman handed the parcel to Nat. She and Butman stood watching his proceedings.

Nat sat down in the grass and carefully went through the old volumes. Between the leaves were bank-notes to the value of several thousand dollars.

"I told ye he meant well," said Nat.

EDWIN LASSETER BYNNER.

For the Companion.

MY STORY.

By Helen Keller.

[Written wholly without help of any sort by a deaf and blind girl, twelve years old, and printed without change.]

Mind, mind alone
Is light and hope and life and power!

I was born twelve years ago, one bright June morning, in Tuscumbia, a pleasant little town in the northern part of Alabama. The beginning of my life was very simple, and very much like the beginning of every other little life; for I could my eyes, and for several days my kind physician thought I would die.

But early one morning the fever left me as mysteriously and unexpectedly as it had come, and I fell into a quiet sleep. Then my parents knew I would live, and they were very happy. They did not know for some time after my recovery that the cruel fever had taken my sight and hearing; taken all the light and music and gladness out of my little life.

By and by the sad truth dawned upon them, and the thought that their little daughter would never more see the beautiful light or hear the voices she loved filled their hearts with anguish.

But I was too young to realize what had happened. When I awoke and found that all was dark and still, I suppose I thought it was night, and I must have wondered why day was so long coming. Gradually, however, I got used to the silence and darkness that surrounded me, and forgot that it had ever been day.

I forgot everything that had been, except my mother's tender love. Soon even my childish voice was stilled, because I had ceased to hear any sound.

But all was not lost! After all, sight and hearing are but two of the beautiful blessings which God had given me. The most precious, the most wonderful of His gifts was still mine. My mind remained clear and active, "though fled fore'er the light."

It took a long time for the "Frost King" episode to dim enough so that Helen could be persuaded to write another story. This one, for the *Youth's Companion,* ended with, "Every day brings me some new joy, some fresh token of love from distant friends, until in the fullness of my glad heart, I cry, 'Love is everything. And God is love!'"

THE
SILENT  WORKER.

| VOL. VII. | TRENTON, N. J., MAY, 1895. | NO. 9 |

Written for THE SILENT WORKER.

THE VOLTA BUREAU

Founded by the Illustrious Inventor of the Telephone—Its Purpose—Some Interesting Facts Connected Therewith.

THE city of Washington, after a long period during which it seemed to have no special character of its own, unless it were as an embodiment of the abomination of desolation spoken of by Daniel the prophet, has of late years grown into a centre of intelligence, so that the streets and avenues radiating from its numberless squares and parks suggest the nerves of a nation throbbing with messages to and from the ganglia in which the experience of the race is being recorded. The Congressional Library, the Medical Museum and Library, the Smithsonian, the Observatory, are outward and visible signs of this great civilizing

credit alike to the heart and to the head of its projector—has been added to these landmarks of intellectual progress. The Volta Bureau, named after one great electrician by its founder, who is also a great electrician, is devoted, not primarily to electrical research, but to "the increase and diffusion of knowledge relating to the deaf." The origin of the Bureau and the reason for its name are as follows: The Emperor Napoleon I, who, we should remember, was no less a promoter of the arts of peace than a great conqueror, established by the French government, from time to time, to any person who should make a discovery or invention of such exceptional value and interest as to deserve extraordinary recognition. This, the Volta prize as it is called, after the eminent Italian philosopher Alessandro Volta, is of the value of

four times since its foundation. In the year 1880, this prize was awarded to Dr. Alexander Graham Bell, for his invention of the telephone and other work in the field of electricity. Being in no need of the money, Dr. Bell determined to make this sum an honor to himself not only in the way in which he received it, but in the purpose for which he should use it. He therefore transformed this "Volta Prize" for the discoveries of his genius into the "Volta Fund" for the promotion of a work which had enlisted his generous sympathies —that of advancing the state of knowledge in regard to the deaf.

Prof. Alexander Melville Bell, the father of the founder, added the sum of $15,000 to the endowment of the Bureau, and the subsequent gifts of the younger Dr. Bell, though not made with any publicity, must amount to a very handsome sum.

tains thirty-nine titles, among which are the Histories of American Schools for the Deaf, and the volumes containing "Facts and Opinions Concerning the Deaf," as presented to the British Royal Commission—two of the most interesting and important works on the subject of the deaf that have ever appeared, and which owe not only their publication, but their origin to the Bureau.

Over twenty thousand copies of these various publications have been sent out to schools, libraries, and persons specially interested in educational, scientific and philanthropic work. Both in America and in Europe the publications of the Bureau and the works for which it has been the medium of exchange are very highly valued by all interested in studying the deaf.

The library of the Bureau contains over fifty thousand reference cards

Photo. by Kirchner.

A. G. Bell   W. A. Mills
C. W. Ellis   Laura Symonds
A. W. McCurdy   Mrs. A. G. Bell   Bessie Appleby   Mrs.
John Hitz   J. C. Gordon   David Bell
A. M. Bell   Mary Symonds   Mrs. Hood
Mary I. Barton   Annie M. Sullivan   Mrs. David Bell   Mrs. Amelia Bell   Bertha Ellis
Elsie Bell   Helen Keller   Marian Bell   Geo. W. Gordon   Douglas McCurdy   Roland Ellis

This was a picnic with friends—Dr. Bell, his wife and father, and his secretary, John Hitz, who was later to succeed him as head of the Volta Bureau. Hitz (standing second to the left) introduced Helen to the New Church doctrines of Emanuel Swedenborg, about which Helen later wrote a book called *My Religion*.

Swedenborg interpreted the Bible in terms of making Christianity a living reality on earth, stressing that divine life is love and men are dead unless they are animated by it. He described the abandonment of self as another name for heaven, with self-will as the cause of the torment of hell.

47

HOME JOURNAL
BOSTON
A PAPER OF TO-DAY

OLD SERIES, VOL. 49. } NEW SERIES, VOL. 10. } No. 49.   BOSTON, SATURDAY, DECEMBER 5, 1896.   PER ANNUM, $2.50. SINGLE COPIES, 5 CENTS.

Helen had long since become a magazine cover girl, a world figure, "a miracle." The Queen of Rumania, under her nom de plume, Carmen Sylva, wrote to her about a plan to resettle Rumania's blind in one city to be called "Vatra Luminosa," and she wanted Helen to promote and raise funds for it. Helen felt the idea of segregation was wrong, that the blind should live among normal people and try, as much as possible, to lead normal lives. She also received letters from the Queens of England, Spain, Greece, and the Netherlands.

Public attention reached the point where a middle-aged, heavy-set woman was found near Helen's home dipping her hands in the lake where Helen had just bathed.

The press interviewed Helen on everything. Asked whether she was a Republican or a Democrat, Helen answered: "I am on the fence. I must study civil government, political economy, and philosophy before I jump."

Asked about the controversy over financial policy based on gold or silver, she said "Well, I think I should be glad to get as much of either as I want."

Helen went to the Wright-Humason Oral School in New York for two years for advanced lessons in oral speech and lip-reading. She still had a toneless voice. When she read aloud, her speech lacked variety and modulation, registering with too much breath in two or three middle tones.

In preparation for college, Helen entered the Cambridge School for Young Ladies in October, 1896. Teacher sat with her in classes, spelled the lectures into her hand. Only the German teacher, and the principal, Arthur Gilman, learned the manual alphabet well enough to talk to her. Since there were still many books unavailable in Braille, Helen had to copy her Latin into Braille so she could recite with the other girls. But for the first time, in school she had friends of her own age who could see and hear. She involved herself in their discussions and games, even played blindman's buff.

Earlier she had written, "I find that I have four things to learn in my school life here—and indeed in life—to think clearly without hurry or confusion, to love everybody sincerely, to act in everything with the highest motives, and to trust in dear God unhesitatingly."

(copy)

                              Cambridge, Mass., July 10, 1897.

My dear Mr. Gilder:

          It is easy to induce me to let you know Helen's
success.   She took "nine hours" of examinations.   The subjects were English, History, French, Elementary German, Advanced German and Latin.   Harvard requires its candidates to pass
in sixteen hours, as you know.   Twelve of these are called
"Elementary" and four are "Advanced."   The examinations may
be divided into two parts, or taken entire at one time;   but
not less than five hours must be passed at the first examination to make "a record."   Seldom does a fellow take an advanced subject at his preliminary examination, but, you see, Helen
had one advanced subject at these, her preliminaries.

About her school work, Helen said, "It was necessary for me
to write algebra and geometry in class and solve problems in physics,
and this I could not do until we bought a Braille writer."

[A Braille writer has six keys. By pressing different combinations
at one time—in the same way that one plays a piano chord—the
writer makes a character at a time in a sheet of thick paper.]

"I could not follow with my eyes the geometrical figures drawn
on the blackboard, and my only means of getting a clear idea of
them was to make them on a cushion with straight and curved
wires which had bent and pointed ends. I had to carry in my mind
the lettering of the figures, the hypothesis and conclusion, the con-
struction and the process of the proof."

To complicate matters, Braille books were being printed in five
different prints for the blind: New York Point, American Braille,
European Braille, Moon Type, and Line Letter.

She had resolved to go to Radcliffe College "because they didn't
want me at Radcliffe and I was stubborn by nature." To the chair-
man of the academic board at Radcliffe, she wrote: ". . . I realize
that the obstacles in the way of my receiving a college education
are very great—to others they may seem insurmountable; but, dear
Sir, a true soldier does not acknowledge defeat before the battle."

49

There was even time to try a ride on a tandem bicycle. She told her Cambridge classmates that she enjoyed it, but still preferred the horse.

Before this ride, a friend offered to buy her a tandem, and she wrote him: "The truth is, I know very little about bicycles. I have only ridden a 'sociable,' which is very different from the ordinary tandem. The 'sociable' is safer perhaps than tandem; but it is very heavy and awkward, and has a way of taking up the greater part of the road." As an afterthought, she added, "I ride with a divided skirt and so does my teacher."

What she loved most about her friend Mark Twain was that he never catered to her, never curbed the roughness of his language because of her presence, although sometimes he would tell her, "Now, Helen, I must curse"—and gently remove her hand from his lips.

Always he was quick to her defense. When a guest spoke with horror of the dullness of Helen's life, "every day the same and every night the same as the day," Twain answered angrily, "You're damned wrong there; blindness is an exciting business, I tell you; if you don't believe it, get up some dark night on the wrong side of your bed when the house is on fire and try to find the door."

And to her, he would say, "Helen, the world is full of unseeing eyes, vacant, staring, soulless eyes."

She met him first when she was fourteen, told him that *Life on the Mississippi* was her favorite adventure story, read the twinkle of his eyes in his handshake and several of his best stories from his lips. He even offered to teach her billiards.

"Oh, Mr. Clemens," she said, "it takes sight to play billiards."

"Not the kind of billiards we play around here," he said.

It was Mark Twain who sparked the fund-raising to help provide for Helen's college education.

The curious wanted to know her technique of finger-reading the manual alphabet. Helen explained that she didn't feel each letter any more than a seeing person saw each letter separately when he read something. "Constant practice makes the fingers very flexible," she said, "and some of my friends spell rapidly—about as fast as an expert writes on a typewriter."

Of course, Helen also knew how to work a typewriter—even a Greek typewriter.

Cambridge, Mass., October II, 1896.

My dear Mr. Gilman;

You can have no idea of how delightful and interesting my first week at the Cambridge School has been! I cannot help thinking of it as the beginning of the fulfilment of a long-cherished dream. When I was quite a small child, I visited Cambridge with my mother and teacher, and they told me about Harvard College; and I remember that I said very decidedly, "I shall go to college some day!" I have always wanted to know a great deal about books, and people, and this wonderful, beautiful world, which is our home. Last summer I used to sit on the porch in the soft sunshine, and let my thoughts make pictures of what my life in Cambridge would be. Now these delightful dream-pictures are being realized, and my studies are more interesting than even Fancy had painted them.

I have made the acquaintance of quite a number of the girls, and now they are learning to spell on their fingers; so that I have the prospective pleasure of being able to talk with them. Of course they make laughable mistakes at first; but that does not matter.

"So the right word be said,
And life the sweeter made."

I need not tell you that my home-life is full of brightness. You must have seen Friday evening that Love reigns supreme at Howell's house.

Now I must say goodbye. Please give my love to dear Mrs. Gilman, and believe me,

Lovingly your friend,

Helen Keller.

Latin.. Hale. Caesar

English - College Eng.   ·· 4

                                          ·· 4

Eng Hist. Dwight   ·, 16

Advanced German. Grote   · 4

Arithmetic - Interpercentage on - Byrne. — 4

                                          ___

                                          20 periods

                                          10 hours =

                                          1/2 the time
                                          in School.

What Qualities Make a Noble Man,
and a Great King.

"A noble man!" What do I mean by "a noble man?" I certainly
do not necessarily mean a man of high rank, power or wealth, as
the Romans did; but, to my mind, a noble man is he who strives to
attain that which is beautiful and imperishable-- love. Love is
the foundation on which all nobility must rest. If a man has love
in his heart, it will find its expression in many beautiful qualities, such as patience, courage and charity. He is patriotic,
honest and firm; he labors, not for promotion, but for the sake of
the good which his work will bring to those around him. He is a
true friend, whom all can trust, and all that is beautiful and
good calls forth his warm enthusiasm. In a word, he is always
"valiant and true."

A truly great king possesses all these qualities, and many
others, which are necessary in the dischargement of his many
arduous duties. He will be self-controlled, clear-headed and
quick to perceive the right thing to be done, and the best way of
doing it. He will be strong, honorable and just; he will respect
all the sacred things of life, such as liberty, property and education; and he will encourage the pursuits of peace-- science,
art, literature, agriculture and so forth. When he fights, it
will be to defend his country against its foes, not for the sake
of conquest or vengeance. In short, he will be "like unto the
King of kings."

Such a man, and such a king was King Alfred of England. He
did not seek his own glory or fame; he had but one ambition, and

that was to leave his people better and happier than he found them. After having driven out the Danes, who had for many years been ravaging and plundering the country, he first gathered the wisest, best men from all parts of his dominion around him, and then he set to work patiently to establish law, justice and order in the land. He rebuilt the old monasteries, and founded new ones, so that the people might learn to read and write, and gain useful knowledge; he himself translated some of the best books he could find from Latin into English. Consequently history tells us that he was the best and most beloved king England ever had.

                                                    Helen Keller.

ἔχει ᾿οικίᾱν μῑκράν.

᾿Οικίᾱ μῑκρᾱ.   ᾿Οικίαι μῑκραί

October 22α, 1897.

This morning I spent two hours or less in showing Helen the key-board of her new type-writer that she is to use in her Greek work. I first showed her the position of the lower-case keys. These she went over twice. Then we took up the upper-case keys. These we went over twice. Then we took up the "figures," going over them also twice. Then Helen asked me if she might write a sentence. I asked her to give me the Greek for Small house and small houses. She wrote the four words just above these lines, having previously practiced by trying the three words at top of the page. I gave her no help or suggestion about the position of the keys or the proper words.

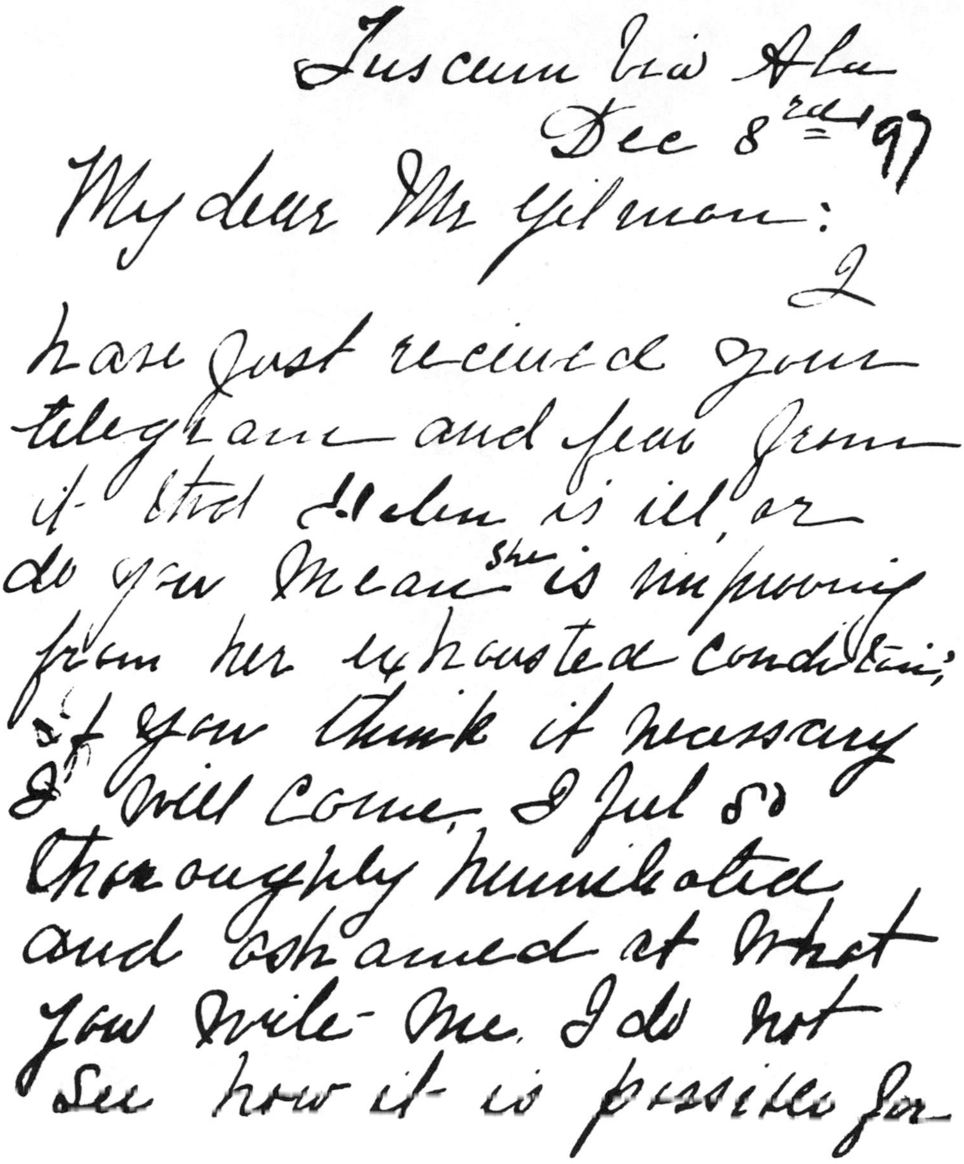

Tuscumbia Ala
Dec 8ᵗʰ 97

My dear Mr Gilman:

I have just recieved your telegram and fear from it that Helen is ill, or do you mean ˢʰᵉ is improving from her exhausted condition; if you think it necessary I will come, I feel so thoroughly humiliated and ashamed at what you write me. I do not see how it is possible for

There was friction between Mr. Gilman and Teacher. Mr. Gilman insisted that Helen was doing too much, and should lengthen her stay at Cambridge School. Teacher felt Helen was working within her capacity and should continue the planned schedule. Mr. Gilman protested to Mrs. Keller, appealing to her on the basis of Helen's health.

Helen's mother seemed convinced by Mr. Gilman, and in her answering letter wrote, "I am unwilling to trust Miss Sullivan's judgment with regard to Helen any further."

Mr. Gilman, meanwhile, had summed up his case, putting full blame on Miss Sullivan, even using the word "cruel."

It soon reached
a point of crisis
. . .

Form No. 44.

NIGHT MESSAGE.
THE WESTERN UNION TELEGRAPH COMPANY.
—— INCORPORATED ——
21,000 OFFICES IN AMERICA.   CABLE SERVICE TO ALL THE WORLD.

This Company TRANSMITS and DELIVERS messages only on conditions limiting its liability, which have been assented to by the sender of the following message.
Errors can be guarded against only by repeating a message back to the sending station for comparison, and the Company will not hold itself liable for errors or delays
in transmission or delivery of Unrepeated Night Messages, sent at reduced rates, beyond a sum equal to ten times the amount paid for transmission ; nor in any
case when the claim is not presented in writing within thirty days after the message is filed with the Company for transmission.
This is an UNREPEATED NIGHT MESSAGE, and is delivered by request of the sender, under the conditions named above.
THOS. T. ECKERT, President and General Manager.

NUMBER   SENT BY   REC'D BY   CHECK

3   Ra Bw   8 Paid Nite

RECEIVED at   Dec 8   189

Dated   Tuscumbia Ala

To   Arthur Gilman
          Concord Ave
You are authorized to act
as helens guardian
          Kate A Keller

Mr. Gilman got his telegram of authority, insisted that Miss Sullivan accede to his
wishes . . .

Miss Sullivan wired Mrs. Keller, "We need you."

When Mrs. Keller came, saw what she had almost done, and sided again with Teacher, Mr. Gilman tried to backtrack in his letter to Dr. Bell. But Helen was taken out of his school and tutored at home.

School House   -   -   34 and 36 Concord Ave.
Margaret Winthrop Hall   21 Chauncy St.
Howells House   -   -   37 Concord Ave.

Mr. Arthur Gilman, Director.

THE CAMBRIDGE SCHOOL
FOR YOUNG LADIES
No. 36 Concord Avenue.

Cambridge, Mass., January 30, 1898.

My dear Dr. Bell:

My feeling towards Miss Sullivan is expressed in the article that I wrote for the Annals. I have no ill-feeling towards her, and it is far from my ~~wish~~ desire to keep her from any ~~interest~~ share that ~~she wishes, or that~~ her friends wish for her, in the Fund that is growing in New York. While I entertain these sentiments, I am more interested in Helen, and I am not able conscientiously to say that I favor any plan that binds Helen to Miss Sullivan for life.

She called Alexander Graham Bell her oldest friend.

He told her the story of the Atlantic cable and started her study of science. He told her of Charles Darwin.

"What did he do?" asked Helen.

"He wrought the miracle of the nineteenth century," said Dr. Bell.

Dr. Bell afterward told Helen that someday there would be an air service between New York and London, plane hangars on top of tall buildings, and even a war in the air.

It was Dr. Bell who asked her to feel a telephone pole:

"What do the vibrations mean to you—anything?"

"Does it hum all the time," asked Helen.

"It is singing the story of life," said Dr. Bell, "and life never stops."

Discussing Shakespeare with Helen, and the line "There is a tide in the affairs of men," Dr. Bell said, "Helen, I do not know if, as these lines teach, we are masters of our fate. I doubt it. The more I look at the world, the more it puzzles me. We are forever moving toward the unexpected.

"Your limitations have placed you before the world in an unusual way. You have learned to speak, and I believe you are meant to break down the barriers which separate the deaf from mankind.

"It is not you but circumstances that will determine your work. We are only instruments of the powers that control the universe. Remember, Helen, do not confine yourself to any particular kind of self-expression. Write, speak, study, do whatever you possibly can. The more you will accomplish, the more you will help the deaf everywhere."

Helen was not the only one Dr. Bell inspired.

When asked what kept her to her dedication, besides her love for Helen, Anne Sullivan said, "I think it must have been Dr. Bell—his faith in me."

Helen entered Radcliffe in 1900, when she was twenty years old. Again, a big obstacle was a lack of Braille books on the various subjects. Teacher not only spelled the lessons in her hand but helped look up words in French, Latin, and German dictionaries.

"In Latin," she wrote John Hitz (whom she called her "foster father"), "I am reading Horace's odes. Although I find them difficult to translate, yet I think they are the loveliest pieces of Latin poetry I have read or shall ever read." From Schiller's play, Helen developed a tender reverence for Joan of Arc, "her undaunted faith in the midst of betrayal and cruelty." She could not see what good could result "from the ruthless destruction wrought by the Alexanders, Caesars, and Napoleons, but my imagination glowed as I beheld Socrates fearlessly teaching the youth of Athens the truth, and drinking the fatal cup rather than surrender."

To somebody surprised at her knowledge of languages, she said, "Why? I know them from the inside."

"Philosophy taught me how to keep on guard against the misconceptions which spring from the limited experience of one who lives in a world without color and without sound."

She learned why mercury is called quicksilver by trying to pick it up after she dropped some.

To her sister, Helen wrote:

"I detest grammar as much as you do; but I suppose I must go through it if I am to write, just as we had to get ducked in the lake hundreds of times before we could swim!"

She soon discovered that college was not the romantic paradise she had dreamed. She couldn't take notes during lectures because her hands were always busy listening, via Teacher. She had to jot them down when she got home. She was increasingly worried about Teacher's eyes. Teacher read books to Helen five or more hours a day (holding the books so close that they almost touched her eyes). The ophthalmologist, Dr. Morgan, heard of it and said, "Oh my God, that is sheer madness, Miss Sullivan. You must rest your eyes completely." He warned her of the danger of permanent blindness. "Your health is more important than Helen Keller's education." "I could have embraced him for that," said Helen.

After that, when Teacher asked Helen if she wanted certain passages reread, "I lied and declared that I could recall them," said Helen. "As a matter of fact they had slipped from my mind."

Reading Kant, Helen learned that "Sensations without concepts are barren, and concepts without sensations are empty."

". . . I put more thought into my senses. I examined as I had not before my impressions arising from touch and smell and was amazed at the ideas with which they supplied me . . ."

Most of her teachers seemed "as impersonal as victrolas." The only professor who took the trouble to learn the manual alphabet in order to talk to her was her German instructor, Dr. William Allan Neilson, who later became President of Smith College. In her classrooms, she felt practically alone. "The professor is as remote as if he were talking through a telephone."

The thing she objected to most was the lack of time.

"I used to have time to think, to reflect, my mind and I. We used to sit together of an evening and listen to the inner melodies of the spirit which one hears only in leisure moments. ". . . But in college there is no time to commune with one's thoughts."

She and Teacher lived at 14 Coolidge Avenue in Cambridge, in a part of what once had been a fine mansion, hidden by huge trees and surrounded by beds of pansies, geraniums, and carnations. Nearby was the home of James Russell Lowell. Once, earlier, they found time to visit another poet, Oliver Wendell Holmes, and Helen recited for him Tennyson's:

"Break, break, break,
   On thy cold gray stones, O Sea!"

"But then I stopped suddenly," she said, "I felt tears on my hand. I had made my beloved poet weep."

Helen loved poetry, and one of her classmates, Bertha Meckstroth, learned to write Braille and copied for her Elizabeth Barrett Browning's *Sonnets from the Portuguese.* None of her other classmates learned to talk with her, but they did make her vice president of their class and pulled her into their hen sessions, where they popped corn, ate chocolate eclairs, and sat around an open fire while they tore apart society. "We stripped everything to the naked skeleton," said Helen. "We were passionately independent."

Once they brought her to a place which she promptly recognized as a kennel and a dog rushed up to her and the girls asked if she liked him. "Take him home, then," they said to her. "He is a gift to you." He was a Boston terrier named Sir Thomas Belvedere. She promptly renamed him "Phiz."

O f all the arts, sculpture meant the most to Helen. She could feel the freedom and the grace and curves. When she touched the Winged Victory, she felt the sweep of the sea winds in its robes. "Of course," she said, "my fingers cannot get the impression of a large whole at a glance; but I feel the parts and my mind puts them together."

Once examining a bas-relief of singing girls, Helen said, "One of them is silent." And so she was—her lips were closed.

Helen even tried to do her own sculpturing but without much success.

W hat could music mean to her? The experts decided it meant mainly beat and pulsation—partly a tactile recognition of sound when its waves hit her, partly the rhythm coming from the vibration of solid objects, the piano or instrument she touched, or from the floor through her feet.

More than anybody, Professor Charles Townsend Copeland of English 22 at Harvard helped develop the potential in her writing. Helen acknowledged this early:

"I am confident that I could go on writing themes like those I have written," she wrote Copeland, "and I suppose I should get through the course with fairly good marks; but this sort of literary patchwork has lost all interest for me. I have never been satisfied with my work; but I never knew what my difficulty was until you pointed it out to me. When I came to your class last October, I was trying with all my might to be like everybody else, to forget as entirely as possible my limitation's peculiar environment. Now, however, I see the folly of attempting to hitch one's wagon to a star with a harness that does not belong to it. . . .

"Henceforth I am resolved to be myself, to live my own life, and write my own thoughts when I have any. . . ."

Out of those ensuing themes grew her book, *The Story of My Life*. Commenting on Helen's writing, Copeland said: "In some of her work she has shown that she can write better than any pupil I have ever had, man or woman. She has an excellent 'ear' for the flow of sentences."

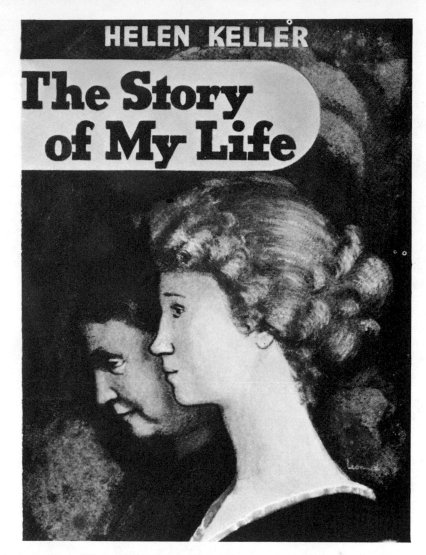

HELEN KELLER

The Story of My Life

Helen's book, published in 1902, while she was still at Radcliffe, confirmed her international reputation of growing greatness. (She also wrote another book, *Optimism,* a brave statement of defiance of people's pity, which won little acclaim.) *The Story of My Life* promptly became a classic; it is published in some fifty languages and seldom out-of-print.

Close friends properly placed the credit. The first part of the book was Helen's story, pieced together from her English themes and delicately edited by John Albert Macy, a handsome young teacher with flowing hair and radical ideas who was later to become a noted critic and author of *The Spirit of American Literature.* He also wrote a supplementary account of Helen's education, and edited letters from her and Anne Sullivan, which were included in her autobiography.

Quick to comment was Mark Twain, who wrote to Helen: "I am charmed with your book—enchanted. You are a wonderful creature, the most wonderful in the world—you and your other half together— Miss Sullivan, I mean, for it took the pair of you to make and complete a perfect whole."

Of the many fine reviews of the book, one of the most perceptive was in the *New York Sun.* It said in part:

"It is perhaps worth reminding the readers that the wonderful feat of dragging Helen Keller out of her hopeless darkness was only accomplished by sacrificing for it another woman's whole life, and if ever the attempt is made in another similar case, it must be at the same cost."

73 Dana Street, Cambridge.

Fay House, Radcliffe.

Fay House, Radcliffe.

terior, 73 Dana Street, Cambridge.

It seemed like an ordinary graduation exercise. But the dean, in his speech, said, "Shall the eyes of the blind be unopened and the ears of the deaf be unstopped?" It was the largest class Radcliffe had graduated up to that time, ninety-six girls.

When the name Helen Keller was called, graduating *cum laude,* Miss Sullivan mounted the steps with her, hand in hand. It was Teacher's triumph, too. As one girl said, Radcliffe should also have given Miss Sullivan a degree.

A French newspaperman reported that the audience broke into "thunderous applause" when Helen and Teacher walked to the platform, but Helen Keller said later, "I felt no thunder of wild applause."

Long before, Teacher had told her, "Helen, you will be glad when you recall the merciless prodding to which I sometimes subjected you."

This was the moment for it, this was their moment.

Copyright, 1905, by the Whitman Studio

AN APOLOGY FOR GOING TO COLLEGE

By HELEN KELLER

ILLUSTRATED WITH PORTRAITS

I is heresy in our time to intimate that a young woman may do better than go to college. Five years ago I had to decide whether I should be a heretic, or adhere to the ancient faith that it is the woman's part to lay her hands to the spindle and to hold the distaff. Some of my friends were enthusiastic about the advantages of a college education, and the special honor it would be for me to compete with my fellows who see and hear. Others were doubtful. One gentleman said to me : "I do not approve of college women, because they lose all respect for men." This argument had, however, the opposite effect to what was intended ; for I thought if our respect for men could be philosophized, or economized, or debated, or booked away, or by any learning rendered null and void, the men must be at fault, and it was my duty as

She was now an established author, getting a fat price for magazine articles. In this one, she remembered, "One gentleman said to me: 'I do not approve of college women, because they lose all respect for men.'"

69

School done, they relaxed with zest—ten-mile tramps over country roads, long rides on their tandem, winter sleigh rides in Shay's express wagon filled with sweet smelling hay, setting supper on the table with the smell of good coffee, sitting in their tree house with their dog Phiz, talking about migrating birds or the jewels of autumn woods. One of Helen's memories of terror was of waiting in another tree house, years before when she was a little girl, while Teacher went for food for lunch.

As Helen remembered it:

"Suddenly a change came over the tree. All the sun's warmth left the air. I knew the sky was black because all the heat, which meant light to me, had died out of the atmosphere. A strange odor came up from the earth. I knew it; it was the odor that precedes a thunderstorm, and a nameless fear clutched at my heart. I felt absolutely alone, cut off from my friends and the firm earth. The immense, the unknown enfolded me. I remained still and expectant, a chilling terror crept over me.

"There was a moment of sinister silence, then a multitudinous stirring of the leaves. A shiver ran through the tree, and the wind sent forth a blast that would have knocked me off had I not clung to the branch with might and main. The tree swayed and strained. The small twigs snapped and fell about me in showers. A wild impulse to jump seized me, but terror held me fast."

And then came Teacher.

They had stayed with friends in Wrentham, and, liking it there wonderfully well, sold Mr. Spaulding's sugar stock to buy a nearby old farmhouse with a neglected field of some seven acres. Teacher converted a dairy room and two pantries into a study for Helen, had a balcony built for Helen's bedroom, with rails that vibrated with the birds' song. In her room she had a plaster Venus de Milo that "foster father" John Hitz had given her, a bas-relief medallion of blind Homer, and curios sent by friends from foreign countries.

They had a steady stream of friends, and discussions were fresh and frank. One of the friends who came often was John Macy, who had helped Helen with her book. He played checkers with her, stretched a wire in the fields to guide her walks, helped her rebuild a stone wall (about which she wrote a long poem, "The Song of the Stone Wall"), took her to a cemetery to feel moss-grown gravestones. He also filled her with a sympathy for strikers, a passion against slums, and a concept of his socialist ideas.

But if John Macy liked Helen, he loved Anne Sullivan.

71

The man who loved them both, Mark Twain, felt that Teacher deserved her full life as a woman—as Helen did. If he saw Helen as a miracle and Teacher as a miracle worker, he saw them first as human beings deserving of fulfillment, and he told them so.

They always enjoyed their visits with him; he always read stories to them. Once, at Helen's insistence, he put on his Oxford gown as Doctor of Letters. And he always described the views to Helen: the snow-covered hill, the dense spruce, the intersecting stone walls.

"Perhaps my strongest impression of him was that of sorrow," said Helen in reflection. "There was about him the air of one who had suffered greatly. Whenever I touched his face, his expression was sad, even when he was telling a funny story."

When John Macy proposed marriage, Anne Sullivan hesitated between love and love: love of John and love for Helen.

What would happen to Helen?

She worried about something else: John was eleven years younger than she was. But she did love him, she did want him.

John Macy agreed to everything. The three of them would live together. Helen would come first. He had a brotherly tenderness for her, and if anything happened to Anne, he would take care of Helen.

Anne Sullivan still hesitated.

After Helen insisted on it, the marriage finally took place on May 2, 1905, in the flower-filled sitting room of their white farmhouse, with Dr. Edward Everett Hale, friend and cousin, performing the ceremony. The Macys went to New Orleans on their honeymoon, and Helen went home, spending much time alone.

lone to walk and wonder of her own future . . .

lone to sit and soliloquize about her own fulfillment . . .

Alone to listen to the lonely murmur of the trees . . .

Alone to hear the restless brooding of the brook. . . .

She knew where the walk ended, how the stones stayed together, what the tree said, where the brook went, but where and what was the future fulfillment of Helen Keller?

Was her future in mere action, mere movement of living?

W̲as her future in her writing?
Teacher wanted her to make her own
decision.

"I am your mother in heart and mind,"
she said, "but I do not own you."

HELEN KELLER INTERESTED IN PHOTOGRAPHY.

Wonderful Blind Girl Engaged in a Literary Work Which She Will Have Illustrated.

The First Appearance on the Lecture Platform of

HELEN KELLER

And her Teacher Mrs. Macy (Anne M. Sullivan)

SUBJECT

"The Heart and the Hand," or the Right Use of our Senses

TREMONT TEMPLE, Boston
ONE NIGHT ONLY

MONDAY EVENING, MARCH 24th, at 8:15 P. M.
SEATS, 25c. to $1.50, NOW ON SALE

DEAF, DUMB, BLIND GIRL NOW CAN SING

Miss Helen Keller Talks on Phone and Tells of Her Engagement to Sing Today

She finally decided to go on a lecture tour across the country, to talk about blindness, about disarmament, about happiness, about the world.

First she had to make her voice more pleasing. Fascinated by her case, Charles White, a voice teacher at the Boston Conservatory of Music, gave her lessons for three years without charge. He came every Saturday and stayed over Sunday. First he learned the manual alphabet so he could talk to her; then he showed her the positions of breathing, how to get the lower ribs and diaphragm involved in freer breathing, how to get the varieties of resonance under the control of the will.

First, control was necessary of the three voice factors—motor, vibrator, and resonator—then, a separate study of vowels and consonants, a use of rhythm accents in speech, an approximation of pitch.

"He would ask me to sing an octave on 'sol' and I did it from my own sense of pitch," said Helen. "Then he asked for an octave one note higher, 'La La.' When I sounded the note, Mr. White struck a tuning fork against the desk. My tone corresponded with that of the fork."

At her first lecture, she forgot all Mr. White's rules, "and felt my voice soaring and I knew that meant falsetto; frantically I dragged it down until my words fell about me like loose bricks."

She went off stage in tears, "Oh, it is too difficult, too difficult. I cannot do the impossible."

78

She continued her lecturing. But she and Teacher needed help.

They were in Bath, Maine, when Mrs. Macy felt suddenly sick. Helen was terrified. She couldn't use a telephone, couldn't find her way downstairs, couldn't explain anything in her queer voice to attendants who came to the door. Mrs. Macy finally managed to call a doctor, and a few days later they headed home.

They found help in a young woman visiting from Scotland who knew little of Helen Keller, less of blindness, and nothing of the manual alphabet. She had no literary streak, but she did have a strong gift for organization. She knew how to read a timetable, plan a trip, keep a schedule, balance a bank account and how to say "No" to time-wasters trying to move into Helen Keller's life via the front door or the telephone.

Her name was Polly Thomson and she came on October 29, 1914.

79

She Condemns Hobble Skirts, Very Low Neck Gowns and Cigarette Smoking, but Enjoys Dancing the Turkey Trot

To some, Helen Keller was a saint; to herself, Helen Keller was a yearning woman. An interviewer asked about clothes, and she said, "Clothes? Of course I like them. Did you ever see any girl who didn't like clothes?" Even in college she had gleefully written her younger sister, "Now we have a swell winter outfit—coats, hats, gowns. We've just had four lovely dresses made by a French dressmaker. I have two, of which one has a black silk skirt, with a black lace net over it, and a waist of white poplin, with turquoise velvet and chiffon, and cream lace over a satin yoke. . . . So you can imagine we look quite like peacocks, only we've no trains. . . ."

She did not like the hobble skirts or the hoops, considered the low neck immodest and unhealthful, and "I think the pointed shoe and extremely big hat are a reflection on the intelligence of women." She also didn't understand why women wanted freedom of the vote and didn't want freedom of their bodies.

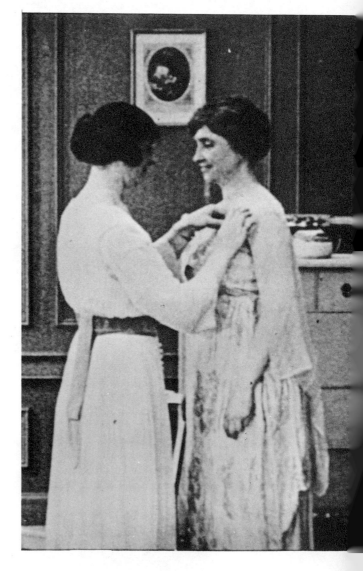

She loved
dancing . . .

● ● ● and knew all the latest fox trot
steps.

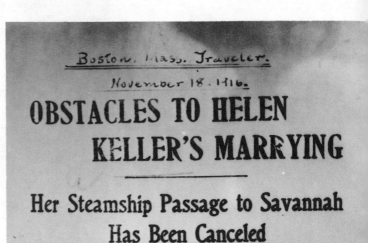

"If I Could See, I Would Marry First of All." -Helen Keller

Miss Helen Keller, blind and deaf college woman and writer, knows exactly what she would do if she could see. Thinking of her as a graduate of two colleges, a writer and a lover of art, one could conceive of her, if suddenly blessed with vision, revolutionizing education, painting pictures or writing sonatas. But she aspires to none of these things.

OBSTACLES TO HELEN KELLER'S MARRYING

Her Steamship Passage to Savannah Has Been Canceled

Her mother (left) said No; Anne Sullivan Macy never knew about it until it was all over.

MRS. MACY HAS LEFT HER PUPIL

Helen Keller Makes Statement About Separation

When the newspapers revealed the story, Helen denied the whole thing. At her mother's insistence a statement of denial was even issued from a lawyer's office.

Outside the world was churning. The threat of war. Woman suffrage. Causes and more causes. Her inward sorrow settled deep, and out of an old shell came a new Helen Keller.

Teacher was on a trip on doctor's orders and wrote Helen:

"I am sorry, dear, that you find it so difficult to write the suffrage article. I should think it would be rather good fun. It is too bad that writing should come so hard with you, especially when it is your only medium of self-expression. I sympathize with you—writing is a lonely, dreary business if you don't love to play with words. But is there any other way you can reach the mind and heart of the public. You are interested in the questions of the day and the handicapped. You desire to serve mankind. How can you do that, except by writing?"

Why Men Need Woman Suffrage

By HELEN KELLER.

(From the Ziegler Magazine for the Blind.)

Many declare that the woman peril is at our door. I have no doubt that it is. Indeed, I suspect that it has already entered most households. Certainly a great number of men are facing it across the breakfast table. And no matter how deaf they pretend to be, they cannot help hearing it talk. Women insist on their "divine rights," "immutable rights," "inalienable rights." These phrases are not so sensible as one might wish. When one comes to think of it, there are no such things as divine, immutable or inalienable rights. Rights are things we get when we are strong race is one of the first to suffer investigation.

The dullest can see that a good many things are wrong with the world. It is old-fashioned, running into ruts. We lack intelligent direction and control. We are not getting the most out of our opportunities and advantages. We must make over the scheme of life, and new tools are needed for the work. Perhaps one of the chief reasons for the present chaotic condition of things is that the world has been trying to get along with only half of itself. We see everywhere running to waste woman-force that should be

Helen Keller Sees Dawn of Freedom in New Woman's Party

By HELEN KELLER.

(Written at Chicago especially for this newspaper.)
(Copyright, 1916, by Newspaper Enterprise Association.)

CHICAGO, Ill. June 8.—For the first time in the history of America women have become a great factor in the selection of a presidential candidate and the creation of a party's platform. They are seen everywhere in Chicago in these convention discussions. Where a very few years ago their appearance would have caused untold comment, now their influence is affecting every "deal" that the politicians are making. Greatest of all, they have just formed a "woman's party," the birth of which I saw as it started winging its way down the ages.

What does all this mean?

What message does this hold for the women of America—of the world?

Helen accepted the criticism. She would write. But she would also use the power and publicity of her public image to help the causes she believed in. She even took Teacher and Polly Thomson with her in this suffrage parade—even though neither of her dear friends believed much in the cause. Helen believed in a woman's party because, "Women have discovered that they cannot rely on man's chivalry to give them justice."

Of the uncaring flappers, she said, "I'd rather be Helen Keller, blind and deaf, than be one of these girls without a goal."

85

It all started with a letter from Dr. Francis Trevelyan Miller proposing a movie be made of her life. Not only would it make a moral point to a troubled world, but it promised to bring her a great deal of money—perhaps enough to make her financially independent. No more would she have to feel dependent on the generosity of her friends.

It all seemed so possible. And, perhaps, even fun.

The fun started in meeting some of the Hollywood famous. Charlie Chaplin invited her to his studio to "see" *A Dog's Life* and *Shoulder Arms,* and "he seemed as pleased as if I were doing him a favor." He even offered to appear in her movie, "and I wish we had let him do it."

Mary Pickford and Douglas Fairbanks discussed the possibility of Mary making a film about a little blind girl, and giving part of the proceeds to the blind. Mary invited Helen to watch the shooting of one of her pictures, but the players were so intrigued with the way Teacher spelled descriptions into Helen's hand, that they kept fumbling their scenes.

The director worked out a signal system of taps for directing Helen's movements during a scene—walk to the window on your right, hold up your hands to the sun, discover the bird cage. ("I had already discovered the cage five times!")

She found it hard to be natural. And it must have made her swallow hard when somebody spelled into her hand an overheard conversation: "Can't you see that there's been no romance in Helen's life—no lover, no adventures of the heart? Let her imagine a lover and follow him in fancy. The picture will be a dismal failure without excitement."

It was a movie with a lot of symbolism: a battle in which some-body representing Ignorance wrestled with somebody else represent-ing Knowledge—with Knowledge thrown over a cliff but coming back to win. In another scene, Helen was Joan of Arc on a white horse blowing a trumpet for the freedom of the world. It was what *Variety* several decades later would call a box-office clinker. But there was one scene that mysteriously caught fire.

Helen Keller described it in her book *Midstream:*

"The swaying uncertain motion of my body, due to lack of balance, seemed to hypnotize them. They sensed something strange in my bearing and my unseeing eyes. When my feet touched the pavement those near me fell on their knees, and before I reached the middle of the alley, everyone was kneeling without a signal from the director! I stood motionless as a statue for a few terrifying seconds, not knowing exactly what to do. I sensed the hushed and unnatural stillness—the palpitating wall of fear that encircled me. I reached out my hands and touched the bowed heads of those who were nearest me. The contact smote my soul, and the tears rolled down my cheeks and fell upon my hands, and the heads they rested upon. The people around me began to sob aloud and drew closer. I felt them touching my robe and my feet. All the love and pity which until that moment I had been trying to simulate suddenly rushed over me like a tide. I thought my heart would burst, so overcharged was it with longing to lift the weary load of misery beneath my hands. Scarcely know-ing what I said, I prayed as I had never prayed in my life before.

"'Pity us, O God! Pity our helplessness, our broken lives and desecrated bodies! Pity our children who wither like flowers in our hands! Pity all the maimed and marred! We beseech Thee, give us a sign that Thou seest our blindness and hearest our dumbness. Deliver us out of the alleys and gutters of the world. Deliver us from the poverty that is blindness and the denial that is deafness! With our groping hands we pray Thee, break the yoke that is heavy upon us!'"

If there was a human experience, she wanted to taste it, feel it, smell it. Would she like to ride in an open-cockpit plane?

"There was only room for the pilot and me. . . . Sitting in an airplane, I always perceive many sensations. I catch the throb of the motor like the insistent beat of a drum in an orchestra of vibrations. I sense the machine trembling like a thing alive. I feel its straining and tugging upward as the strong winds tug at a tree, and I know when we return to earth by the downward gliding motion of the machine.

"Was I afraid? How could fear hold back my spirit, long accustomed to soar?"

Up, up, the machine bore me until I lost the odors of the flying dust, the ripening vineyard, and the pungent eucalyptus! Up, up, up, I climbed the aerial mountains until I felt rain clouds spilling their pearls on me.

"Then the machine went through amazing dips! I felt in them, as it were, organ music and the sweep of the ocean, winds from far-off mountains and illimitable plains. As the machine rose and fell, my brain throbbed with ecstatic thoughts and whirled on tiptoe, and I seemed to sense the Dance of the Gods."

I had never had such a satisfying sense of physical liberty. . . . Life is either a daring adventure, or it is nothing. . . ."

She loved to ride a horse in summer. "When I ride horseback," she said, "it is not merely as a sport but also as a sort of communion with nature."

● ● ● and a sleigh or toboggan in winter.

"We would get on our toboggan, a boy would give us a shove, and off we went! Plunging through drifts, leaping hollows, swooping down upon the lake, we would shoot across its gleaming surface to the opposite bank. What joy! What exhilarating madness! For one wild, glad moment we snapped the chain that binds us to earth, and joining hands with the winds we felt ourselves divine!"

They camped for two months, with a small gasoline stove, an icebox, and their huge dog, Sieglinde. Passing a river full of logs headed for a sawmill, Helen insisted on crawling into the river, keeping her body out of reach of the logs and clinging to the rocks. "The current turned me over and over like a leaf, but I managed to touch some of the logs as they shot past, and the sense of adventure was wonderful."

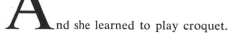

And she learned to play croquet.

oming to the ship launching, she felt the rhythmic thunder of the trip hammers, the driving of the rivets, the vibrations of the huge cranes. It was a hot day and she was thirsty. "As I hurled the bottle, I let escape a profound sigh at the waste of so precious a liquid."

he Stony Tribe made her a sister and Chief Walking Buffalo gave her an eagle feather, which reminded her of an ostrich feather the philosopher William James had brought her "because it is soft and light and caressing."

After refusing the offer for years, Helen finally felt forced to accept an annual pension from the philanthropist Andrew Carnegie. (Carnegie suggested that she should cut in half the $1.50 price of admission to her lectures.)

Helen still searched for other means to support herself. The magazine market seemed to be dwindling. "Nobody cares what I think about the tariff or conservation or the Dreyfus Case," she complained. Anyway, the editors didn't. They wanted her to write only about herself, a subject she felt she had exhausted. "Do not meddle with matters not related with your personal experience," one warned.

Meanwhile, George Lewis wrote a song about Helen Keller called "Star of Happiness," and persuaded booking agents Harry and Herman Weber to meet Helen. The Webers, enchanted with her, immediately proposed a nation-wide vaudeville tour on a contract that offered more money than they had ever made before.

The set was simple: curtains opening on a drawing room with a fire crackling on the hearth, French windows opening into a garden, a vase of flowers, velvet hangings. The act lasted twenty minutes. A circuit tour lasted forty weeks, and the travel, unlike the one-night lecture tours, was not a rat race because they usually stayed a week or so in each city. Here she is at the State Theater in Houston, with Teacher, Polly, her manager (left), and the publicity woman.

It opened with the background music of Mendelssohn's "Spring Song." Then Teacher, with her weak eyes, faced the too-bright lights and told the background of the Helen Keller story. Then Helen herself came out through the parted stage curtains, lightly guiding her steps by stage props of piano and flowers. She spoke briefly on the need for happiness in the world, showed how she could read Teacher's lips and keep time with the piano. Then came questions from the audience:

"Can you really perceive color?"

"Sometimes I feel blue and sometimes I see red."

"Do you close your eyes when you go to sleep?"

"I never stayed awake to see!"

"Do you play any musical instrument?"

"Only the hand organ."

"What do you consider the hardest thing in the world?"

"To get Congress to do anything."

They also wanted to know if she was clairvoyant, could tell time without a watch, ever used a ouija board, ever had any dreams, ever thought of getting married.

(Mark Twain once had told her, "Let us be thankful for the fools. But for them, the rest of us would not succeed.")

She felt intensely conscious of the audience, felt its breath coming to her face in small pulsations. She sensed its wave of sympathy or indifference. She enjoyed visiting theatrical dressing rooms and feeling the various costumes, and many of the performers put on their acts especially for her. Sophie Tucker taught her how to use make-up. "I hope you don't think my songs were too naughty," said Sophie.

"How can anything be naughty that gives joy to so many people?" said Helen.

Outside critics complained that Helen's two-year vaudeville tour was in bad taste and urged that she talk only in schools and churches. The Webers silenced them quickly: "Will you pay her as much as we do?"

One of her admirers was Carl Sandburg:

"I saw and heard you last night at the Palace," he wrote her, "and enjoyed it in a thousand ways. For myself, the surprise was to find you something of a dancer, shifting in easy postures like a good-blooded race horse. . . . Possibly the finest thing about your performance is that those who hear and see you feel that zest for living; the zest you radiate is more important than any formula about how to live life."

Her mother died while Helen was appearing in Los Angeles.

"I received the telegram telling me of her death two hours before I had to go on stage. I had not even known she was ill. Every fiber of my being cried out at the thought of facing the audience, but it had to be done."

One of the questions asked was, "How old are you?" and she answered, "How old do I look?" which got a laugh.

Another asked, "Are you happy?" She swallowed hard at that and answered softly, "Yes, because I have confidence in God."

The great of the world wanted to meet her . . . the actress Ethel Barrymore.

● ● ● the naturalist Luther Burbank, who put her hand very gently on a desert cactus which no living creature can touch without pain and then on a thornless edible cactus he had created.

● ● ● the Hindu poet Rabindranath Tagore—who insisted that women controlled the world's future—read to her in a deep, prayerful voice his poem "I forget, I forget."

● ● ● George Bernard Shaw—whose handshake was unresponsive, bristling, prickly—made a characteristic quip. When told by Lady Astor, "You know, Miss Keller is deaf and blind," Shaw answered sharply, "Why, of course, all Americans are deaf and blind—and dumb."

She even made President Coolidge smile. "I had always heard he was cold," she said, "but there was not the least coldness in his hand." Coolidge placed Helen's fingers on his lips and said, "I am greatly interested in your work and I will cooperate with you in every possible way." He not only became the honorary president of the American Foundation for the Blind, but sent a generous personal donation.

She met President Theodore Roosevelt in 1903, and Roosevelt spelled some letters in her hand, but then said, "I'm too clumsy." He talked about football, and sent her a basket of flowers.

President Hoover greeted her with deful cordiality and unassuming simy, spoke hopefully of the political situaand listened indulgently when Helen him how fearful she was that our ecoc problems would not soon be solved. en she spoke of his terrific labors, he "You don't meet such a dull man as I veryday."

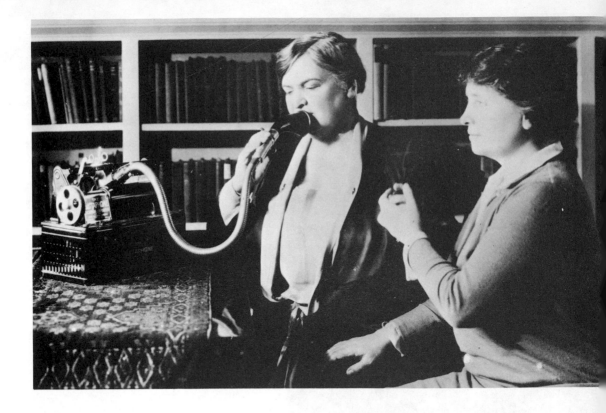

elen Keller's full opportunity for
service really began at the age of forty, a
life dedicated wholly to the blind. It con-
sumed her. Speeches everywhere, lobbying
in Congress for Bill 168 for talking books
for the blind, fund raising, article writing.
She always considered her most important
article on the blind one she had written
earlier for the *Ladies Home Journal* attack-
ing venereal disease in parents as a prime
cause of blindness in children—it was the
first time the subject had ever been mentioned in a national magazine.

The Encyclopedia of Education asked her
to prepare a paper on blindness; the Governor of Massachusetts appointed her to the
Massachusetts Commission for the Blind.

She seriously debated between the deaf or
the blind as a lifework, feeling the im-
possibility of working for both. She only
had one lifetime to offer.

"I am so constituted," she said, "that I
would have worked with equal zest for the
crippled or the poor or the oppressed."

"Guard Your Eyes,"
Helen Keller Urges
Youth of America

Woman Makes
Appeal Direct
the Country.

The Correct Training of a Blind Child
Simple Difference Between Training a Blind Child and One Who Can See
By Helen Keller

HOW TO BE BLIND
Give the Blind a Chance to Become
Self-Supporting, Self-Respecting Citizens
HELEN KELLER

My Future As
By Helen Keller

AND OF THE WORLD
By Helen Keller *The American*
ILLUSTRATIONS BY FRANKLIN BOOTH

Helen Keller
May Sept 1935

"I Must Speak"
A Plea to the American Woman
By Helen Keller

YEAR ago I wrote in THE LADIES' HOME JOURNAL about the prevention of blindness. I wrote guardedly and with hesitation; for the subject was new to me, and I shrank from discussing before the general public a problem which hitherto

to the child's birth she has unconsciously received it through infection from her husband. He has contracted the infection in licentious relations before or since marriage. "The cruelest link in the chain of consequences," says Dr. Prince Morrow, "is the mother's innocent agency. She is made a passive, unconscious medium of instilling into the eyes of her newborn babe a virulent poison

Sincerely yours
Helen Keller

Fund raising was a key concern. This appeal went everywhere, and so did she. For three years, she and Teacher and Polly covered the country, talking to more than 250,000 people at 249 meetings in 123 cities and raising more than a million dollars. Contributors ranged from a Washington millionaire whom she inspired, who gave $100,000, to 15-year-old Bradford Lord, a crippled boy who sent her his savings of $500 and a bouquet of roses, to the smaller children who emptied their piggy banks in her lap.

Helen received a $5000 annual achievement award given by the *Pictorial Review*. Friends begged her to keep it for her own sharp needs, but she donated all of it to the Fund—"for the loneliest people in the world who stare into the dark with nothing but the dark staring back."

Mrs. Franklin D. Roosevelt, whose husband was then Governor of New York, was an early volunteer. Will Rogers broadcast appeals for Helen, sent her money saying, "Don't hesitate to ask for more." Henry Ford contributed generously, told her that his plants employed seventy-three blind men, not for pity but because they did good work. President Woodrow Wilson queried her about her work, but offered no specific help.

Meeting Thomas A. Edison, she said, "If I were a great inventor like you, Mr. Edison, I would invent an instrument that would enable every deaf person to hear." Edison said he considered his deafness a blessing, a high wall to exclude distraction, and, besides, he said, "People say so little that is worth listening to."

Of the blind and deaf, Helen Keller said: "Ours is not the stillness that soothes the weary senses; it is the inhuman silence which severs and estranges. It is the silence not to be broken by a word of greeting, or the song of birds, or the sigh of a breeze. It is a silence which isolates cruelly, completely."

Of the neglected, outcast blind children of the world, she said: "It is to live long, long days, and life is made up of days. It is to live immured, baffled, impotent, all God's world shut out. It is to sit helpless, defrauded, while your spirit strains and tugs at its fetters."

"It is not so wretched to be blind," she said later, "as it is not to be capable of enduring blindness."

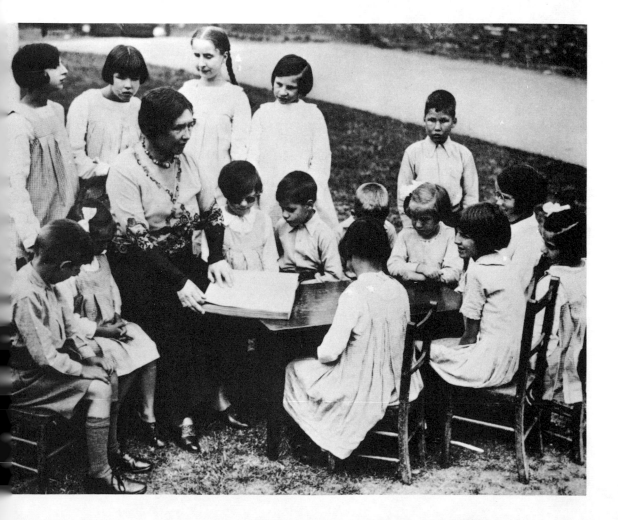

They went to England and Scotland for a vacation, with two trunks, a hatbox, a shoe bag, four large suitcases, three small suitcases, three rugs, and three extra coats.

"No sooner had we arrived," said Helen, "than the air became aquiver with wings as millions of birds rose from their perches—gulls, terns, puffins, sea swallows, and cliff skuas. Their shrill clamor came vibrating through the water to the boat, and I was as startled as the others who heard it. Never in our lives had we been surrounded by such dense masses of feathery clouds shimmering in the morning light.

"I obtained plenty of fish and amused myself holding a morsel high for a gull to catch on the wing. Polly kept saying 'Ready!' as the gulls overtook the boat, and my fingers tingled as a powerful beak jerked the fish away. . . . Everybody said that the gulls, flying so swiftly after a ship, poising with such grace to feed from my hand, were a delight to behold."

Helen got a ride in the train cab—the engineer let her sit in the seat where the Prince of Wales had sat and let her stoke the furnace; she visited a coal miner's family and went 900 feet down a mine shaft; the Earl of Aberdeen broadcast a lecture about her; she learned how to make proper tea and swing a golf club; and the University of Glasgow gave her an honorary degree.

Then Anne Sullivan Macy, now increasingly blind and ill, received a telegram John Macy had died.

"The dreadful drama is finished," Mrs Macy wrote a friend. "There is in the most passionate love more pain than joy."

Scotland was Polly's country. They stayed in a small, quiet cottage called "Dalvien" in West Kilbride near Glasgow. Polly took Helen into the fields they both loved, talked to the farmers, smelled the overwhelming smell of a great harvest, touched the glossy coats and wet noses of curious cows.

Sometime earlier they had sold their house in Wrentham, because they could not afford to keep it up, and they bought an odd-shaped brick house full of peaks and angles in Forest Hills in Queens, New York. They laughingly named it "Castle on the Marsh." Its best feature was a small study for Helen on the upper floor, "open to the four winds of heaven." Helen had started to study Italian in order to read Petrarch and Dante in the original.

They had a small garden: "just a pile of sun, songs, blossoms and butterflies, for what else matters?" Then Helen added complainingly, "It takes two of us to drag the hose around and I get so dirty. . . ."

Their house was always full of company and conversation. Helen could distinguish between a Yankee twang and a Southern drawl by touching two or three spots on the speaker's throat. In a roomful of conversation, if somebody stopped spelling into her hand, she quickly questioned, "What are you talking about?"

"During the gaps when I am left alone," she said, "I amuse myself by observing callers. There is nothing about me to put them on their guard, and I find I can, or imagine I can, substitute myself for the visitor. If he is dull, I know it by the parts of his conversation that are repeated to me. If he is fidgety, I can tell by the behavior of his feet and hands and by the small vibrations that come to me when he laughs to cover his embarrassment.

"I know when callers are pleasant by a sort of spiritual freemasonry. If a woman is sitting beside me, and I read her lips, I at once notice the friendliness or the animation of her face and the little nameless motions of head and hand that give color and emphasis to her words, and I observe her moods, gay and grave."

There were often children in her house, both the blind and the seeing, and she would read to them all.

Thomas Edison had complained about her voice, saying it sounded like "steam exploding" and that he heard only the consonants. But children always have understood her more easily.

Of her own voice, she said, "It is not a pleasant voice, I am afraid, but I have clothed its broken wings in the unfading hues of my dreams and my struggle for it has strengthened every fiber of my being and deepened my understanding of all human strivings and disappointed ambitions."

A big part of her huge mail came from curious school children, many of them asking simple, often silly questions. Helen's friends begged her not to take the time answering them, but she said she could never bear to disappoint a child.

The President of Temple University notified Anne Sullivan Macy that they wanted to give her an honorary degree, as they had given one to Helen. She declined. The President persisted:

"First: I regard Miss Keller as one of the most remarkable personalities now living, and I have always thought that what you have done with her was little if any less remarkable than what she was able to do for herself. . . . To put it vulgarly, she was inside seeking to look out, whereas you were outside looking in. You could not have had the same longing for the light that she had."

At Helen's insistence, Teacher accepted the degree. When, at the graduation ceremony, Helen still got the public attention, Teacher said smilingly, "Even at my coronation, Helen is queen."

What a blind-deaf person needs is not a teacher," wrote some-one, "but another self."

Professor Albert Einstein once told Anne, "Mrs. Macy, your work has interested me more than any other achievement in modern education. Not only did you impart language to Helen Keller, you unfolded her personality, and such work has in it an element of the super-human."

A questioner wanted to know: "If you had your life to live over again, would you follow the same path?"

"Would I be a teacher?" Anne said. "We do not, I think, choose our destiny. It chooses us."

Anne was impetuous, enthusiastic, not always logical, bored by the commonplace, ("it was a lifetime struggle for her to be kind to dull people"). She loved perfection and nonsense, "and was a porcupine of principle." Since her first trip north with Helen in 1888, Captain Keller had been unable to pay her salary—and she never told Helen. Of her early poverty and degradation, she told Helen nothing until she was sixty-four and Helen was fifty. She loved beauty, once spent all of her slim teacher's salary on a velvet fur-lined cape. A series of operations failed to help her dwindling sight and sapped all her strength. The pain was such that she often told Helen, "How I shrink from this day!"

And once, sobbing, she said, "I am trying so hard to live for you."

"Teacher, you must get well," said Helen, and an unperceptive friend added, "Without you, Helen would be nothing."

"That would mean that I have failed," said Teacher sadly.

7111-112ᵀᴴ STREET
FOREST HILLS, NEW YORK

November 24, 1936

Dear Mrs. Powers:

The birds are gone. The life that throbbed through tree, bush and grass is stilled. The ground is frozen so that it hurts our feet to tread on it. Yet we thank God for the seed-time and the harvest that have vanished, for the rough, steep ways that again lead to beauty and fertility.

Even so it is winter in my life since the guardian angel of fifty years no longer walks by my side on earth. Yet I thank God for the wondrous gift He has withdrawn a little while, and for the difficulties to be overcome that shall be my tribute to Anne Sullivan Macy.

Out of the darkness in which she died and I still am living I thank you, O friend, for the joy of lending a helping hand to those whose eyes seek light in vain. I thank you for gifts of faith and support that have renewed their courage, transmuted their shipwrecked lives and sweetened their hearts with the sense of accomplishment. Strengthened by your good-will we shall press on to new goals, and obstacles that once were our despair shall be sign-posts pointing to a life richer than any we have dared to dream. May God's blessing rest upon you for your generosity to the American Foundation for the Blind, whose activities comfort the sightless with the rod of counsel and the staff of self-help.

Blessing you for your loyalty to us in past years, I am

Gratefully yours,

Helen Keller

Mrs. Fred Perry Powers
Alden Park, The Manor
Germantown
Philadelphia, Pennsylvania

110

In her journal, Helen wrote:

"... the month in the hospital during which she hung between life and death ... her piteous eagerness to get home. I ache all over as I remember how she grew thinner and thinner. I was glad she could not see my swimming eyes as I massaged her and noticed skin and bones where I had once felt the softness of her chest and shoulders. ...

"... her darling hand growing cold in mine ... the smell of opiates heavy in the room ... sorrowing friends who drew me away so that her body might be prepared for the funeral. ...

"... later when I touched not Teacher's blessed face but fixed features from which expression had fled. I feel again the recoil, the cry that escaped me, 'It is not Teacher ... It is not Teacher. ...

"When she breathed no more, somehow the faith she had wished she could hold with me rose up stronger than ever, and leaning forward, I said, 'You know, dearest, don't you, that life is beginning over again, glorious with light and peace.'

"The body is only the shadow of the soul."

MRS. MACY IS DEAD; AIDED MISS KELLER

Teacher and Famous Blind and Deaf Pupil Associated Since They Met in 1887.

SHE KEPT IN BACKGROUND

In Recent Years Her Sight Failed and Younger Woman Heroically Looked After Her.

Shortly before Teacher's death, Helen Keller wrote: "I have been frequently asked what I should do without her. I smile and answer cheerfully, 'God sent her and if He takes her, His love will fill the void,' but it terrifies me to face the thought that this question brings to my mind.'

"The day I hold dearest of the year is the day she came to me. . . . I cannot picture anyone else in her place. . . . My education was accomplished in the tragedy of my Teacher's life. She understood the void in my soul because her childhood had been so empty of joy."

Anne Sullivan Macy was buried on November 3, 1936, in the National Cathedral in Washington, not far from the tomb of Woodrow Wilson; the Bishop of Washington called her "one of the great teachers of all time."

Alexander Woollcott went even further. Asked by school children "Who, in your opinion, is the greatest living woman?" he answered immediately, "Anne Sullivan Macy." In his opinion she was still alive.

112

My last memory of Teacher as I knew her, was on an October evening . . . she was laughing while Herbert was telling her about the rodeo he had just seen. She spelled to me all he said, and how tenderly she fondled my hand. Her dearness was without limit, and it was almost intolerable. Beautiful was her touch—the creative flame from which sprang the joy of communication, the power of love binding me to my kind, and the intelligence that quickened new senses within my limitations. Afterward she drifted into a coma from which she never awoke on earth."

Then, thoughtful, Helen said, "People think Teacher has left me, but she is with me all the time."

A stranger wrote: "I know, dear Helen Keller, your heart is crying out as mine is for the loved one, and our only comfort is to do what good we can in the world."

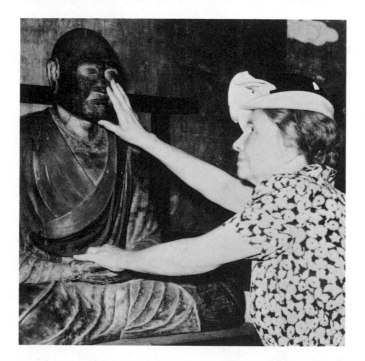

There was much to do. The world's uncared-for blind were waiting.

Teacher's last request had been, "I beg you, Helen, to promise me that after I am gone, you and Polly will be light-bringers to the handicapped of Japan."

Takeo Iwahashi, one of the great workers for the blind in the Orient, told Helen that there were some 100,000 deaf and 160,000 blind in Japan and only 4000 of them were being taught.

Helen quickly got busy preparing and memorizing a dozen different speeches of appeal. She kept writing and rewriting them "until I felt mentally black and blue." "And," she added in her journal, "they must be as short as possible if I am not to over-tax my listener's patience with my halting delivery; and I am anxious to put over as many worth-while ideas as I can."

After an interlude, she wrote, "For the life of me, I have not been able yet to memorize all the speeches. I am almost in despair. I can practice only an hour and a half without getting hoarse, and this does not give time for more than four or five speeches.

"I find the others have slipped out of my mind as if on roller skates, and I swear silently and relearn them. Are they worth all this trouble, I wonder, and will my message impress the Japanese sufficiently to bear practical results?"

But she was convinced of one thing: "I have resolved that I shall not risk paralysis by shaking every hand extended to me or grow dumb by talking from breakfast until midnight each day in Japan. I have frequently been asked if it tires me to talk, and I have replied, 'Did you ever hear of a woman who got tired talking?' I am that woman for once, today!"

J apan opened everything to her. She
was the first woman permitted to touch the
great bronze Amita Buddha at Daibutsu. In
Tosa province, they let her handle the famous white bird with an eighteen-foot tail
that had taken two hundred years of cross-
breeding to produce. The bird normally
stayed high in a tree so that its tail could
hang freely, and a page boy exercised the
bird for a half hour each day holding the
tail to keep it from touching the ground.

They played their old instruments for her.
On the koto, they played a composition by a
blind musician. "What a cascade of dainty
notes fell on my hand, as raindrops on
autumn leaves. Every now and then a
startling cry of distress burst from the
quivering instrument. Shriller and sadder it
rose, then sank into soft wistfulness."

But her main time was spent in speech-
making and fund raising, and, before she
left, she had raised forty million yen for the
Japanese blind and deaf.

B ack in Forest Hills, Helen told Polly, "I can never get used to this house without Teacher."

Teacher's desk was still there, her chair, her books, ("Her bed is gone," Helen noted, "and that is a relief, for it was a bed of pain. . . .").

Helen traveled into Manhattan on the new subway.

"I was glad of the subway ride," she said, "and I shall take one as often as possible coming home. I like any mode of transit—subway, elevated, or the bus—that brings me into closer contact with people. Polly describes their faces or their talk. Through the sense of smell, impressions tell me much—powder, perfume, tobacco, shoe polish. I also sense freshness and good taste in odors of soap, clean garments, silks, and gloves. From exhalations I often know the work people are engaged in because the odors of wood, iron, paint, or the office cling to their clothes. In an automobile, I miss these intimate revelations of how my fellow creatures live."

Soon afterward, Dr. Robert Pfeiffer, a biblical scholar in the Harvard Divinity School, invited them to make use of his empty house in Westport, Connecticut. His uncle, a trustee of the American Foundation for the Blind, later supplied much of the funds to help build a new house for Helen and Polly nearby, in 1939.

There were horses nearby, and she loved horses. Polly never left her. "In the nature of things," wrote Helen, "I would never feel that anyone could really take Teacher's place, but Polly's deep integrity gave Teacher confidence that the fine ligament of sympathy between her endeavors and mine would never be broken."

There was some time now for new experiences   . . . a football game.

There had always been time for old experiences renewed. Years before, when famous violinist Jascha Heifetz played Schumann's "Song of Moonlight" for her, she wrote:

"My fingers rested lightly on his violin. At first the bow moved softly over the strings, as if the master were questioning the Spirit of Music what he should play for one who could not hear. The bow fluttered. From the sensitive instrument there came a tremulous faraway murmur. Was it the faint rumor of the wings of birds? Each delicate note alighted on my finger tips like thistledown. They touched my face, my hair, like kisses remembered and lovelit smiles. Immaterial, transient as the sigh of evening winds, the violet breath of dawn. Are they rose petals dropped from a fairy's hand, or wordless desires born in the heart?

"There is a change of mood. The bow is lifted to the point of radiant flight. The melody rises like Shelley's skylark, climbing the air like voice and wing challenging immensity. The song is joyous and yet nowhere is there a loneliness so great as the little bird in that vast dome of light, for the moment, the only actuality in the universe, yet so slight a thing, a glimmering echo of thought, a passionate prayer, a dauntless faith in things unseen."

118

Martha Graham invited her to "feel" a dance rehearsal done especially for her.

She listened to radio concerts, her fingers lightly on the speaker; she distinguished between the oboe, piano, and harp; and recognized at least one of Beethoven's symphonies. She disliked jazz. It had a bombarding sensation not pleasant to her touch, and disturbed her emotions. "When it continues for some time," she admitted, "I have a wild impulse to flee."

[At an actual concert, a marble floor prevents her feet from feeling the music, although she can catch some chords by placing her hands on the chair.

A reviewer of a Toscanini concert of the NBC Symphony Orchestra remarked that he saw Helen Keller sitting upon a small board platform at the rear of the sound-proofed studio, the vibrations reaching her by means of the wooden sounding board beneath her feet.]

Therefore, she felt free to write, "I am blind—yet I see; I am deaf—yet I hear."

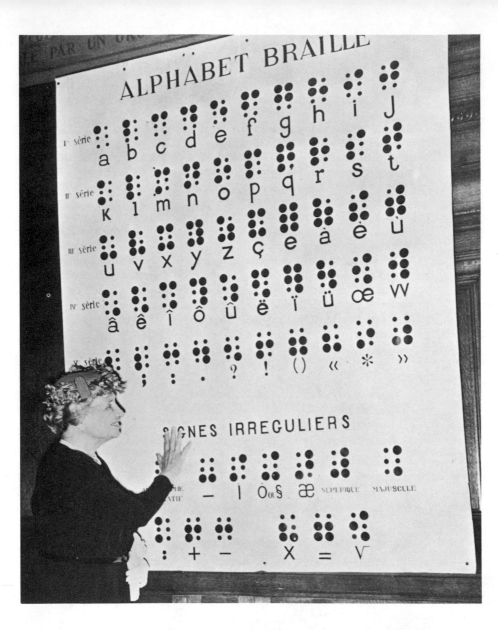

In 1952, the centennial of Louis Braille, Helen wrote movingly of the magic of his six dots and their sixty-three combinations that provide "the golden key that opens the prison door" of the dark world.

"I use Braille as the spider uses the web," she wrote, "to catch thoughts that flit across my mind."

One of her friends who used the same spider web for the same aim of service to the world blind was Peter J. Salmon, Executive Director for the Industrial Home for the Blind in Brooklyn. Salmon established the first Vocational Institute for the Blind, pioneered the first vocational placement service, and set up service models in many fields for the world blind.

Her world travels slowed, but never halted because the need of the blind always stared at her. She made this personal comment on travel: "When I go from one place to another, I leave suddenly the surroundings that have become familiar to me through touch and daily association and I cannot readily orient myself in a strange locality. I am conscious of the same kind of remoteness one senses out at sea, far from all signs of land; and on my first tours, this feeling was quite oppressive."

But the children were always waiting . . . in France . . .

● ● ● and England . . . and everywhere.

She once wrote, "I dream of a little child that plays and play hide-and-go-seek with me, though we never succeed in finding each other because a mist always rises between us. . . ."

One thing she hated wherever she went—hotels. They were the only places where she felt "painfully aware of the lack of personal liberty, which, next to idleness, is the hardest part of being blind."

So, whenever she could, she stayed in houses with friends . . .

● ● ● shopped for her French bread like everybody else.

I n England Winston Churchill wanted to meet her . . .

124

In India, Prime Minister Nehru was enchanted by her . . .

She paid deep tribute at Mahatma Gandhi's shrine . . .

Satisfied the feminine impulse by dressing in a sari . . .

126

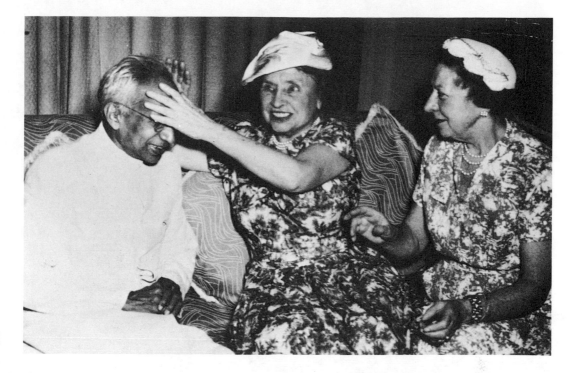

F elt the face of India's famous philosopher-statesman, Vice President Sarvepalli Radhakrishnan . . .

● ● ● who told her, "You have been a source of inspiration to me. I was a psychology student and read in your life how will power can overcome circumstances."

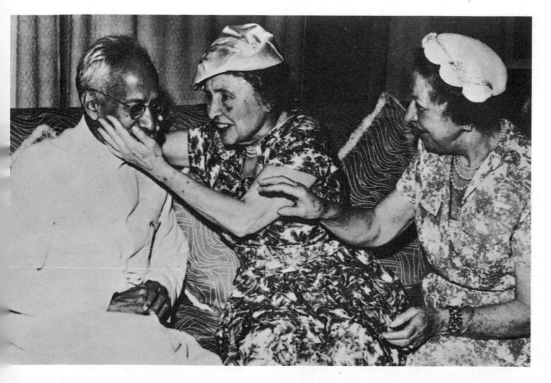

127

She handled koala bears in Australia . . .

● ● ● and a carabao in the Philippines.

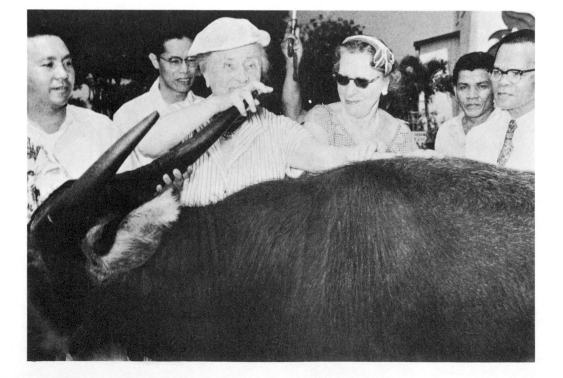

S he touched the wheat in Israel . . .

● ● ●   and the sphinx in Egypt.

She wore a costume in Korea . . .

●●● and a flowered lei in Manila. Of leis, she wrote, "Their blended fragrances intoxicated me—gardenia, peko-kee (very much like scented wisteria), plumeria, mock orange—so that I forgot the weight and heat of the flowers on my neck."

But when she entered her hot stateroom and found leis piled high on her bed, "I could have screamed. I was so surfeited with sweet smells and crazy to stretch out. I simply threw the wreaths on the floor. I understood as I had never before the pain-ful effect of a dazzling spectacle too pro-longed upon the eyes of those who see."

That night she dreamt of being smothered with sweetness.

The meetings seemed countless. "When they try to talk to me," she said, "and find their words have to be spelled into my hand, their tongues cleave to the roofs of their mouths, and they become speechless. And I am quite as uncomfortable as they are."

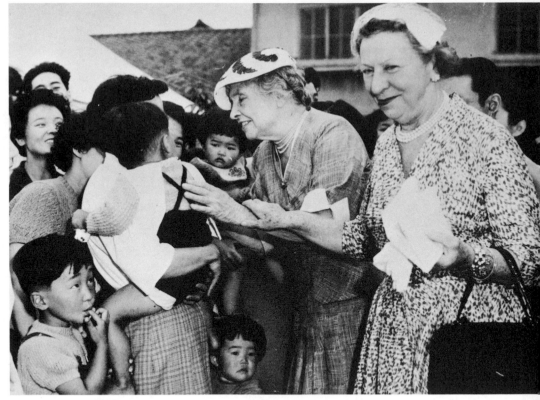

But this was a strangeness she never felt with children.

To the little blind girl, Helen Keller was a storybook inspiration . . .

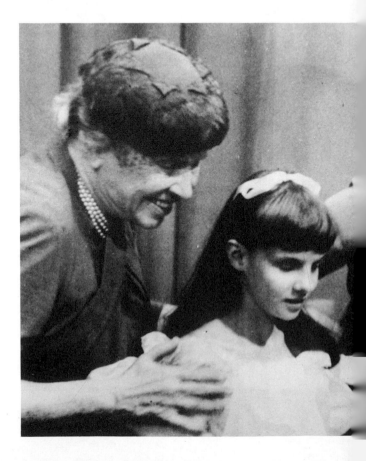

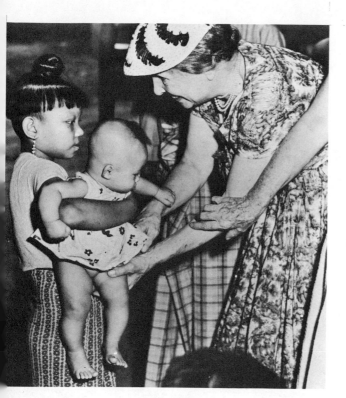

To a fat little Siamese baby,
she was a warm, loving hand.

She saw the African problem as a human problem, a world problem.

This world tour took five months, over 40,000 miles. But was only one of many.

At the end of it, a reporter asked her to define love: "Love? Wl bless you, that's easy; it is what everybody feels for everybody else

uring World War I, she had visited the blinded soldiers at U. S. General Hospital No. 7 in Baltimore, and one of them said to her, "Gee, I read about you in school, but I never thought then I'd be blind myself."

She didn't try to buoy them with false optimism. She explained the future difficulties and loss of personal liberty, but she did tell them the compensation of books, friends, and work. She was her own best walking testimonial that happiness was possible.

One wounded soldier offered her one of his eyes if it would make her see.

"I Deny That I Am Blind," Says Helen Keller in Message to Wounded Boys

Miss Helen Keller, famous deaf and blind woman, who also was dumb until she taught herself to speak, and who in a remarkable interview says: "It is not what we are or touch or feel which makes us happy, but that which we think and feel and do."

135

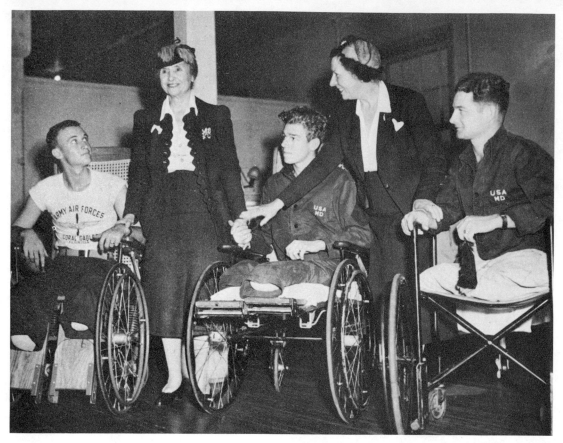

During World War II, she toured the hospitals with a similar message.

She remembered one particularly bitter, angry blind soldier to whom she said, "I once raged with anger. I was rebelling against my handicap."

He softened and said, "But the Braille dots only feel like sandpaper to me."

She held his hand and answered, "Your hand will grow softer and more sensitive with time."

She was asked: "Does it not make you sad, taking all these hands scarred with pain and fatigue?"

"No," she said, "I love the courage throbbing through them."

Somebody wrote a poem about her:

Fools, they! They call her blind!
They call her blind, yet she can lead
A thousand soul-sick men
From cold gray stones and make
   them heed
The song of wind and rain.

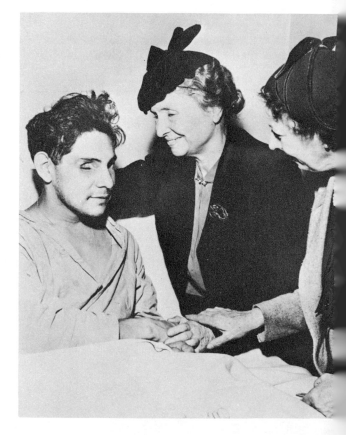

She remembered how much she loved to dance . . .

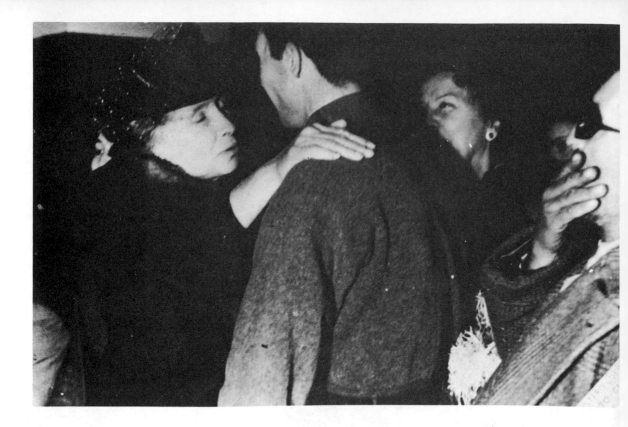

● ● ● and her enthusiasm made a blind soldier happy, too.

She had a report to make to the people. She quoted a blind lawyer, Marcel Bloch, who had said, "Lack of sight is not our chief difficulty, but lack of understanding and co-operation in our struggle for rehabilitation."

And she added: "No one knows—no one can know—the bitter denials of limitation better than I do. I am not deceived about my situation. It is not true that I am never sad or rebellious. But long ago, I determined not to complain. The mortally wounded must strive to live out their days cheerfully for the sake of others. That is what religion is for—to keep the hearts brave to fight it out to the end with a smiling face."

When the actor Joseph Jefferson once explained to her what the bumps on her head meant, saying of one:

"That is your prize fighting bump."

"I never fight," she replied, "except against difficulties."

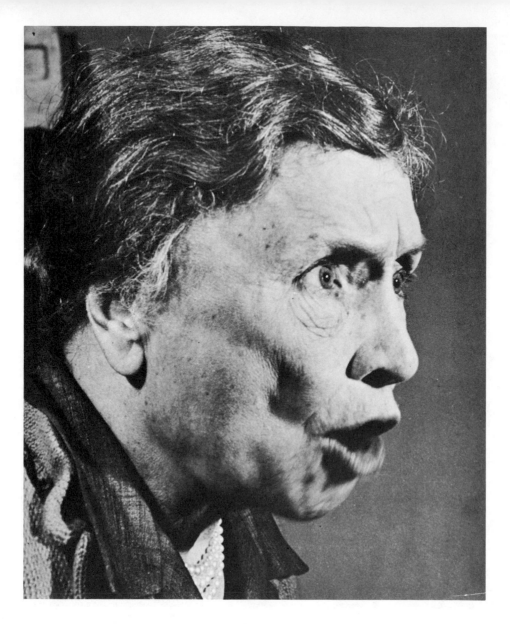

She summed up a personal complaint:

"A gust of irritability is blowing through me just now because there has been a recurrence of a tendency in some people to try to run my affairs. This seems all the stranger to me because since I was seventeen I have arranged my own life. At the age of twenty-two I began working very hard for whatever money I have earned the past thirty-four years. Of my own accord I have undertaken public responsibilities in America and other lands. After Teacher's health broke down I worked very much alone, with Polly's hand to furnish information and her voice to reinforce my halting speech.

"Yet there are still those who appear to think it incumbent upon them to alter my life according to their own ideas! There was some excuse when I was young and bewildered in the search for something worth doing. But Mother and Teacher knew me better than anyone else ever did, and they never dictated the course of action I should follow. There have always been other friends with power to advance the work for the blind, and they respect my desire as a human being to be free."

News came to her in Rome, in the midst of another world tour, that their house in Westport, "Arcan Ridge," had burned to the ground. All that was left was some silver that had been removed, and a few half-burned scattered sheets of an unfinished poem. Most tragic of all was that the fire had destroyed the manuscript of the book she had started on, *Teacher,* almost three fourths completed—

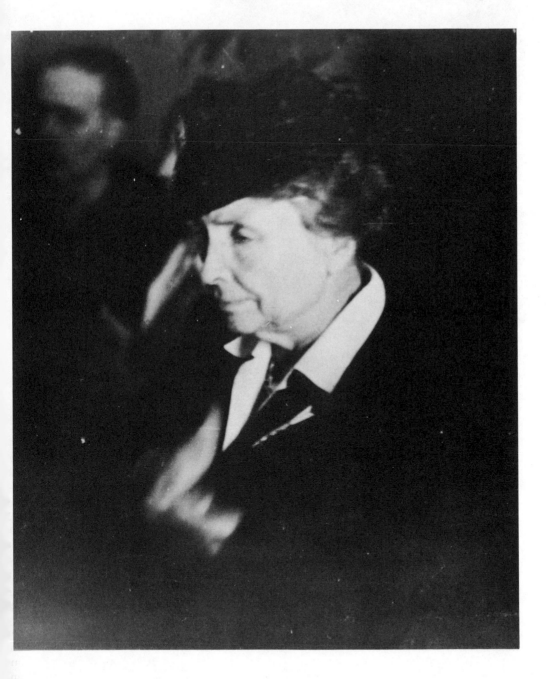

But this book, *Teacher,* was a book she had to write, and she started all over again.

She found a letter she had written to Teacher in March, 1917: "Dearest Teacher,

"Just think, last Friday was my soul-birthday, and I had to spend that day of days away from you! Do you realize it? Thirty years ago you came to a quiet village, you, a young girl alone in the world handicapped by imperfect vision and want of experience—you came and opened life's shut portals and let in joy, hope, knowledge, and friendship. . . . God bless you my teacher from everlasting to everlasting. . . ."

And she found a note in her journal made during one of her trips:

"When I awoke this morning, I started to find Teacher to tell her somehow my joy that the world had been blessed in her birth. Then I remembered and was transfixed with pain. There was no language for my longing to see her—to keep not merely reaching out through aching heartbeats but to be with her and a part of her other home where joy is in its fullness. . . ."

And she found a poem she herself had written:

> Teacher, and yet again
> Teacher—and that was all.
> It will be my answer
> In the dark
> When death calls.

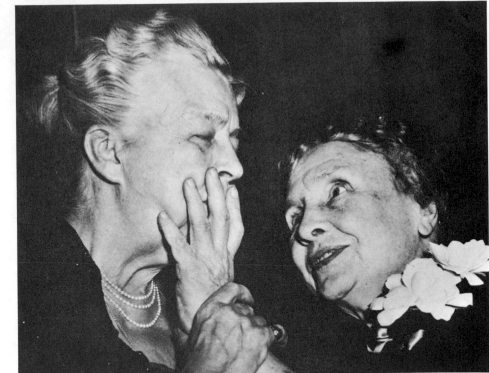

B̲ut she had many friends. Mrs. Roosevelt . . .

● ● ● and, one of the most intimate, Katharine Cornell, of whom Polly Thomson
said, "She is the only one with whom I would leave Helen alone."

She had first met Franklin Delano Roosevelt when he lent encouragement during the hard early years of the American Foundation for the Blind. She felt "upon his worn face shines the heroic ambition of Hercules to subdue the beasts of greed and deliver the earth from robber states." She remembered being in a room when a phone rang to tell of President Roosevelt's death and how "the room went mute and limp."

She had met President Harry Truman, too, and found an open hand—"there are no crooks in his fingers." And she remembered how he was in tears when she spoke to him.

And she loved President Eisenhower's smile.

Jo Davidson had learned the manual alphabet from a deaf friend, also a sculptor, and persuaded Helen Keller to come and pose for him at his Pennsylvania farm. She later paid him high tribute:

"Until I came to your studio," she wrote him, "I had often seemed to move in a deaf-blind show, but you multiplied my powers of feeling, reflecting, and observing how you worked, and now there will be a new significance in whatever there is left for me to accomplish."

"You confirm the truth which has always burned in me—spiritual exaltation is not enough. We must also lift our earth horizon or we shall always profane our high thinking by mean living."

They became close friends. She and Polly vacationed in an old manor house in Tours that belonged to the Jo Davidsons, and there she celebrated her seventieth birthday among the cornflowers, poppies, and cherry trees, while Jo Davidson painted a portrait of her and Polly.

While in France earlier, she had examined Rodin's famous "Thinker": "Primal, tense, his chin resting on a toilworn hand. In every limb I felt the throes of emerging mind. I recognized the force that shook me when Teacher spelled 'water' and I discovered that everything had a name and that the finger motions were the way to whatever I wanted. Often before had my deliverance caused me to wonder, but not until then had I perceived clearly how Teacher hewed my life bit by bit out of the formless silent dark as Rodin hewed that mind genesis out of the rock."

But long before that, Jo Davidson had said to her, "I've got a surprise for you. I want you to meet someone." And he let her feel his sculptured picture of her.

F riends helped rebuild their house in Westport. The pantry had an electric buzzer connected with Helen's second-floor study to tell Helen when meals were ready or when guests had arrived. The bells' vibrations came to her on the desk and she stamped her feet on the floor to indicate she was coming down.

Away from her own home, unless she was given guide points, it took her several hours to examine a room, and she was never really sure she had covered all of it. At home, nobody moved anything without letting her know, because she orients herself by contact with furniture. Her bewilderment is complete when the rugs are taken up for cleaning, and she has to relearn her whole pattern because she has a poor sense of distance—doesn't know when she has reached the door until she has come to it; and she is entirely without a sense of direction—often starts towards the opposite wall instead of the door.

The fence is her guide rail, and in the winter, when it is covered, her daily walk becomes a daily adventure.

"I think people do not usually realize what an extensive apparatus the sense of touch is," she said. "It is apt to be confined in our thoughts to the finger tips. In reality, the actual sense reigns throughout the body, and the skin of every part, under the urge of necessity, becomes extraordinarily discriminating. It is approximately true that every particle of the skin is a feeler which touches and is touched."

Here is her description of a walk through the fields.

"With the nerves of my body, especially on forehead and face, I know by air currents whether the path is opened or closed by trees. . . . The wind registers a different temperature as I climb or descend. . . . I know when I enter a wood because the ground for a distance is covered with mold or pine needles and the shade on my face is different from the breezes alternating with sunshine on the road."

Dogs are her friends, and they have always been with her. A great Dane, a Shetland collie, a fat Lakeland terrier, a Scottie. She had buried Phiz, her Boston terrier, long ago under a beautiful white pine. Siegelinde, the great Dane, another favorite, once stood with her paws on Teacher's shoulders licking her face and drawing one of her soft ears gently across Teacher's eyes, as if she knew they were sick eyes. And the time a policeman in Boston had shot one of her dogs, Helen had said softly, "If he had only known what a good dog she was, he wouldn't have shot her."

I love to follow dark roads that smell of moss and wet grasses, hill roads and deep valley roads so narrow that the trees and bushes touch me as I pass.

"I love to stand on a little bridge and feel the brook flowing under it with minnows in her hands.

"I love to sit on a fallen tree so long that the shy wood things forget it may be imprudent to step on my toes, and the dimpling cascade throws water spray in my face. With body still and observant, I hear myriad sounds that I understand—leaf sounds, grass sounds, and twigs creaking faintly when birds alight on them, and grass swaying when insects' wings brush it, and the thistle's silvery flutter. These sounds I hear, yet my way is still."

Someone asked her how she knows the difference between night and day. "Oh," she said, "in the day, the air is lighter, and there is more motion and more vibration in the atmosphere. In the evening quiet, there are fewer vibrations. The air is dense and one feels less motion in things."

Of all the things that grow in my garden, I love best the evergreens. . . . They stretch out their branches like hands to me and tease me and pull my hair when I pass them. In the springtime when the world swims with odors of life they bend toward me like friends full of glad news. If I could fathom that murmur, that sigh. . . ."

How did she think of colors? She said she thought of red as warm; she connected pink with rosebuds and green with young, growing plants. Purple means to her deep feeling; yellow means joyousness, gaiety, sunlight; blue means space, distance, airiness, the sky.

Pink is "like a baby's cheek or a soft Southern breeze." Gray is "like a soft shawl around the shoulders." Yellow is "like the sun. It means life and is rich in promise."

For Helen, there are two kinds of brown. One is warm and friendly like leaf mold." The other is "like the trunks of aged trees with worm holes in them, or like withered hands."

I had not dreamed what abundance of physical enjoyment I possessed until I sat down and tried to express in words the lacy shadows of little leaves, the filmy wings of insects, the murmur of breezes, the tremulous flutter of flowers, the soft breathing breast of a dove, filaments of sound in waving grass, and gossamer threads intertwining and unreeling themselves endlessly.

"A gentleman asked me what beauty meant to my mind. I must confess I was puzzled at first. But after a minute I answered that beauty was a form of goodness—and he went away."

Her desk is her own haven. Nobody touches her papers. She knows exactly where everything is. If she wants to find any Braille notes she's thrown in the wastebasket, she digs them out herself, folding them against her chest, fingering them until she finds what she wants.

Her normal working day: six or seven hours, seldom interrupted by anybody. An exception was the time—at a friend's house—when they rushed in to tell her of some fresh bear signs under a pine tree near the house, and out she went.

She can't go back to correct typing mistakes, so she makes notes to the editor indicating corrections in previous copy. There are a minimum of these.

She has her own checkerboard and plays, here, with Mr. M. Robert Barnett, Executive Director of the American Foundation for the Blind. The squares on her checkerboard are so cut that the men stand in them firmly. Black checkers are flat, and red ones curved, on top. Each checker has a hole in the middle for a brass knob to distinguish the king from the others.

In her chess set, the white chessmen are larger than the black.

In catching a conversation, she moves her hand quickly to see "the twist of the mouth" that indicates to her a tone in the voice . . .

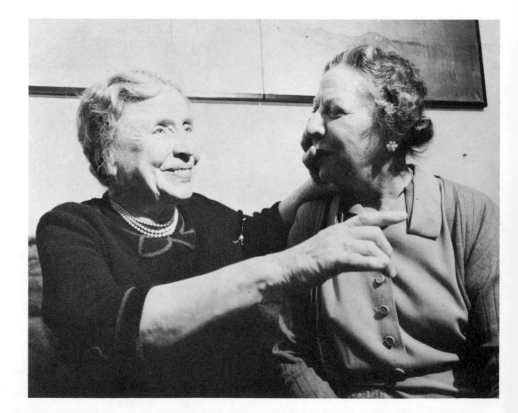

● ● ● or a twinkle in the eye.

She has an acute sense of humor. Of her constant examinations by curious specialists, she said, "I wonder if any other individual has been so minutely investigated as I have been by physicians, psychologists, and neurologists. I can think of only two tests I have not undergone: so far I have not been vivisected or psychoanalyzed."

Of her constant interviewers, she adds: "I assure them that I know day is not night and that it is no more necessary for me to have raised letters on the keys of my typewriter than for them to have the keys of their piano lettered."

Of cocktail parties: "I feel certain that these functions have a useful purpose which I cannot understand. Otherwise we should not tolerate the absurdity of shaking hands with hundreds of curious human creatures whom we have never seen and will in all probability never see again."

If Helen Keller lives in a quiet tower, it is nonetheless wide open to the world, and she is always up to date on world events. And she is always the woman to speak her mind: whether it involved the Duke of Windsor's courage in abdicating his throne or the purges in Soviet Moscow, which she compared to the hysterical witchcraft trails in Puritan New England. "Apparently there is the same frenzied fear among the Soviet leaders, and the same determination to force the prisoners to admit crimes they have never committed."

Of the threat of war, she said:

"How could I write with the conflagration of cities blinding my thoughts," and added:

"We need permanent things to soak peace into us as well as progress—the beauty of the earth, seedtime and harvest, the smiles of lovers, the joy of the young in being alive, pride in craftsmanship. Why, oh, why must we let ourselves forget these lasting treasures in an age of consuming ambition, speed, madness, and accumulated goods that leave us no chance to live? If we cannot be contented with a little, no wealth will ever satisfy us. Only from simple beginnings can creation go on unchecked. . . ."

If some news particularly interests her, and she wants to store it in her tactile memory, she swiftly spells it to herself on the fingers of her hand—sometimes unconsciously. Sometimes these fingers flutter as she walks along, thinking and talking to herself.

Polly not only read her the news, but they went to the movies and theater together. Polly spelled out the dialogue, facial expressions, costumes, humor, action. She has always enjoyed this more than reading a play because "then it seems as if I were living in the midst of stirring events. . . ."

She is part of her household. Usually up at five, she clips the garden borders, then makes her bed, goes for her walk, busies herself with making breakfast, helps wash the dishes. . . .

She cracks nuts, brings in flowers from the garden and arranges them by form (not color) beautifully and symmetrically, checks the laundry list. Once, long ago, a fire broke out and Helen smelled the tar and burning wood before anybody, opened a window, and woke her mother and sister, who called the firemen just in time. There is no helplessness in her.

She has a hard concept about beauty in women; their frantic pursuit for physical perfection, she feels, starves their minds and stunts their souls. Helen Keller's concept of the truly beautiful woman is one who has a well-stored mind, poise, strength for serious discussion, and "a gift of blending laughter with fragrance of the heart."

This, of course, had nothing to do with her love for lovely things and her fun in shopping on Fifth Avenue.

"Fifth Avenue," she said, "is a very odorous street. It may sound like a joke to say it has an aristocratic smell, but it has, nevertheless. As I walk along its even pavements, I recognize expensive perfumes, powders, creams, choice flowers, and pleasant exhalations from the houses. I smell delicate food, silken draperies, and rich tapestries. Sometimes, when a door opens as I pass, I know what kind of cosmetics the occupants of the house use. I know if there is an open fire, if they burn wood or soft coal, if they roast their coffee, if they use candles, if the house has been shut up for a long time, if it has been newly painted or decorated, and if the cleaners are at work in it."

Paris to her was a blend of perfume, powder, wine, and tobacco.

"I know when I pass a church whether it is Protestant or Catholic. I know when I am in the Italian quarter of the city by the smells of salami, garlic, and spaghetti. I know when we are near the oil wells, I used to be able to smell Duluth and St. Louis miles off by their breweries, and the fumes of the whisky stills of Peoria, Illinois, used to wake me up at night if we passed within smelling distance of it."

But more than smells, Fifth Avenue was a shopping street, a street of windows for women, and Polly spelled it all into her hand.

Often people stared at them.

"I cannot see people staring at me," she said, "but I am always accompanied by people who can see, and it is embarrassing to them. I am told that in the Orient people avert their eyes when a blind man passes, and the Arabs cover their eyes when they enter his dwelling."

Another time, admirers tore her clothing, snatched flowers from her hat.

But sometimes she encountered real respect, and it made her proud: the cab driver who let her out and then yelled to a passer-by: "Lady, I have just driven Helen Keller!" and the stranger who cleared a way for her near an elevator, saying he thought of her as a saint. He knew she didn't like to be called a saint, "But that's how we feel."

Of course she could go out to a restaurant . . .

● ● ● or a night club.

She once said, "Sometimes I feel as if I were a music box with all the play shut up inside me."

More people could understand her now, but her voice had brought her little of the happiness she had anticipated, though it did bring her a greater sense of freedom. In her dreams, she seldom groped or had any need of a guide but enjoyed self-sufficiency in every crowd.

Independent as she felt, she still, at a New Year's Eve party, nearly burst into tears when she stood up, took hands, and sang "Auld Lang Syne." It was a song she had sung with Teacher throughout the years.

The city was fine, but there was nothing more pleasurable than visiting friends at the seashore (Mrs. Roosevelt, top left; Katharine Cornell, top right and lower center) and going for a ride in a motorboat.

Once she had also enjoyed rowing. "Of course I cannot guide the boat very well," she had said. "Someone usually sits in the stern and manages the rudder while I row. Sometimes, however, I go rowing without the rudder. It is fun to try to steer by the scent of water grasses and lilies, and of bushes that grow on the shore. I use oars with leather bands, which keep them in position in the oarlocks, and I know by the resistance of the water when the oars are evenly poised. In the same manner I can also tell when I am pulling against the current. I like to contend with wind and wave."

And the beach always had a wonder to it.

The first time she went into the ocean as a little girl they had tied a rope around her waist and fastened it to the shore so she could move freely.

She had plunged into the water without fear and "felt the great billows rock and sink. The buoyant motion of the water filled me with an exquisite quivering joy. Suddenly my ecstasy gave place to terror; for my foot struck against a rock and the next instant there was a push of water over my head. I thrust out my hands to gain some support, I clutched at the water and the seaweed which the waves tossed in my face. But all my frantic efforts were in vain.

"As soon as I recovered from my panic sufficiently to say anything, I demanded, 'Who put salt in the water?' "

Back home with her books she could savor her favorite poet, Walt Whitman:

"I began to read his poetry years ago, at a time when I was almost overwhelmed by a sense of isolation and self-doubt. It was when I read 'The Song of the Open Road' that my spirit leaped up to meet him. For me, his verses have the quality of exquisite physical sensations. They wave flowers, they quiver like fountains or rush on like mountain torrents. He sings unconquerable life."

Or Thoreau:

"When I read Thoreau I am not conscious of him or the book or the words which flow under my finger tips. I am There. Through him nature speaks without an interpreter. I am a part of the river, the lake, the field, the woods—I am a spirit wild and free. I have the illusion of being free of my deprivations."

Or *Gone With the Wind:*

"I am glad to see Scarlett being transformed from a spoiled belle into a courageous, responsible worker. Rhett Butler is out of the picture at present, much to my relief. He is one of the sensible people without heart whom I shun as heartily as any fool—he is supremely selfish, sarcastic, and bitter.

"Last night my heart almost stopped when I read in *Gone With the Wind* how Scarlett, finding her mother dead, felt she had come to the end of the road—to a dead wall from which there was no escape. But resolutely I said over and over, "In the Divine Bosom is our dwelling place where all limits vanish!"

She said once of books: "I read with interest every book I can lay my hands on except pocketbooks, checkbooks, and needlebooks."

And when she was a little girl she made Teacher read and reread "Little Red Riding Hood" over and over again, "because I like sad stories."

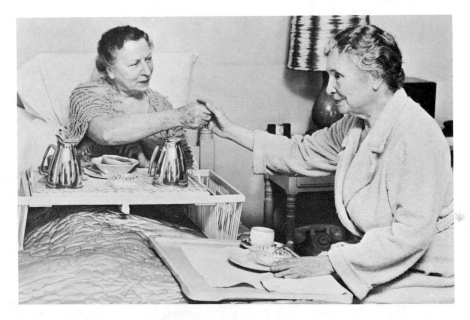

Occasionally she brought up Polly's breakfast tray, most of which Polly had set ready the night before.

Years before, Helen Keller had asked Teacher: "If anything should happen to you suddenly, to whom do you wish me to turn for help? How could I best protect myself against anyone who might not be honest or reliable? Oh, Teacher, how alone and unprepared I often feel, especially when I wake in the night."

The answer, of course, was Polly, a lifetime of Polly.

P olly who told her when the birds were singing; Polly who put her hand on a moss-covered stone or a gushing spring or a little calf; Polly who painted for her imagination the feathery billows of blossoms on the hillsides; Polly who protected her privacy as nobody else possibly could.

173

Polly, who gave her life to serve as one of the three lives of Helen Keller.

174

Polly Thomson, Interpreter, Dies; Eyes and Ears for Helen Keller

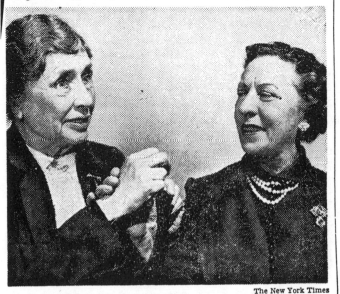

The New York Times

Polly Thomson, right, communicating with Helen Keller

Special to The New York Times.

BRIDGEPORT, Conn., March 21 — Polly Thomson, who for forty-five years had replaced eyes and ears for blind and deaf Helen Keller, died in Bridgeport Hospital late last night. She had been in the hospital since Dec. 1. Her age was 75.

Miss Keller, who is 79 years

"All Polly needed to do was spell out three or four letters of a long word into Helen's hand and Helen would immediately grasp the word.

Miss Thomson came to this country from Scotland to visit an uncle in Swampscott, Mass. Soon after her arrival she met Miss Keller and her teacher, Mrs

BIRTHDAY GREETINGS TO MISS KELLER

On Thursdday afternoon, June 23, the
Senate passed a resolution extending greetings
and best wishes to Helen Keller on the occasion
of her 80 th birthday on June 27.

This is the Text of the Senate's resolution:

Whereas Miss Keller will celebrate her
eightieth birthday on June 27, 1960; and
Whereas this remarkable woman, stricken
deaf and blind in infancy, has for more than
fifty years tirelessly devoted herself to the
battle for the economic, cultural, and social
advancement of the physically handicapped throughout the world, making her own conquest of dis-
abilities a symbol of hope for millions; and
Whereas in her long and faithful association with the American Foundation for the Over-
seas Blind she has traveled to more than a score
of nations throughout the world; and
Whereas in all these travels she has inspired immeasureable progress in services to the
blind, deaf, and the deaf-blind, and has won
countless new friends for the United States of
America and the cause of democracy and freedom
and:

Whereas the Congress and the Chief
Executive have expressed deep concern in the
improvements of conditions among the physically
handicapped, and have initiated constantly ex-
panding programs to this worthwhile end:
Now, therefore, be it
Resolved that, in recognition of the vast
contributions made by Miss Keller
To the well being of all humanity, the
S enate hereby extends its greetings and best
wishes to Miss Keller on the occasion of her
eightieth birthday, which will occur on June 27,
1960.

176

I believe in the immortality of the soul because I have within me immortal longings. . . . I believe in the life to come I shall have the senses I have not had here and that my home there will be beautiful with color, music, and the speech of flowers and faces I love.

"I walk unafraid toward the enchanted wood where the foliage is always green.

"I believe that life is given us so that we may grow in love and I believe that God is in me as the sun is in the color and fragrance of a flower—the Light in my darkness, the Voice in my silence."

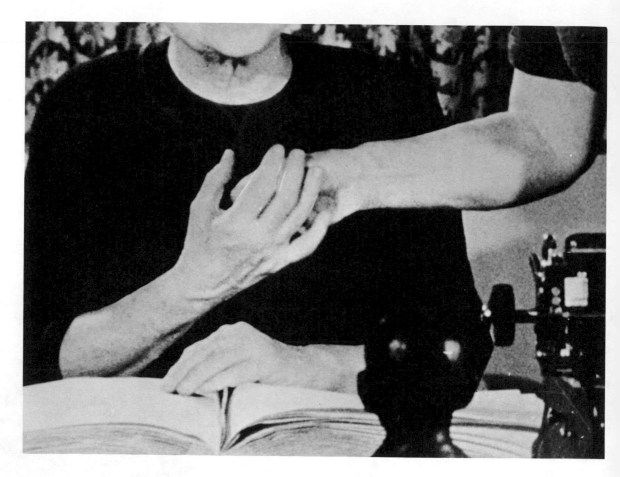

When Helen was just a child, Teacher wrote
a poem called "Hands":

Hands, understanding hands,
Hands that caress like delicate green leaves,
Hands, eager hands,
Hands that gather knowledge from great books—
    Braille Books—
Hands that fill empty space with livable things,
Hands so quiet, folded on a book—
Hands forgetful of words they have read all night,
Hands asleep on the open page,
Strong hands that sew and reap thought,
Hands tremulous and ecstatic listening to music
Hands keeping the rhythm of song and dance.

178

A reporter once asked her:

"Does Helen Keller feel that she has really achieved anything in her life?"

She replied immediately:

"I believe that all through these dark and silent years God has been using my life for a purpose I do not know, but one day I shall understand and then I will be satisfied."

PICTURE CREDITS

The Keller home in Tuscumbia, Alabama. American Foundation for the Blind (A.F.F.B.). Page 25.
Captain Arthur Keller. Kate Adams Keller. New York Public Library (N.Y.P.L.). Page 26.
The room where Helen was born. A.F.F.B. Page 26.
Helen as a child. Perkins School for the Blind (P.S.F.B.). Page 27.
Michael Anagnos. Volta Bureau, Washington. Page 28.
Dr. Samuel Gridley Howe. N.Y.P.L. Page 28.
Laura Bridgman. P.S.F.B. Page 29.
Helen with her dog. N.Y.P.L. Page 29.
Anne Sullivan as a girl. A.F.F.B. Page 30.
The garden house. A.F.F.B. Page 31.
The pump. Library of Congress (L.C.). Page 31.
Helen as a child with Anne. P.S.F.B. Page 32.
Letter from Anne Sullivan. P.S.F.B. Page 33.
Anne Sullivan as a young woman. P.S.F.B. Page 34.
Helen reading. P.S.F.B. Page 34.
Helen's first letter. Page 35.
Title page of report on Helen by Mr. Anagnos. Page 35.
Helen and Mr. Anagnos. P.S.F.B. Page 36.
Sarah Fuller. Volta. Page 37.
Helen and Anne. P.S.F.B. Page 38.
Letter from Helen. P.S.F.B. Page 39.
Helen and friends. P.S.F.B. Page 39.
Helen in 1894. P.S.F.B. Page 40.
The Frost King by Helen Keller. Brown. Page 41.
The Frost Fairies by Margaret Canby. Brown. Page 41.
Helen and her sister. N.Y.P.L. Page 42.
Helen, her mother, Anne, and Dr. Bell at Niagara Falls. P.S.F.B. Page 43.
Helen and Anne. Brown. Page 44.
Helen, in 1899, reading. A.F.F.B. Page 45.
Helen. P.S.F.B. Page 45.
Opening of story by Helen in the *Youth's Companion*. Page 46.
Helen with Dr. Bell and other friends on a picnic. Volta. Page 47.
Cover of *Home Journal* with Helen's picture. Page 48.
Helen at twelve years. A.F.F.B. Page 48.
Letter to Mr. Gilder from Mr. Gilman, about the Radcliffe entrance examinations. P.S.F.B. Page 49.
Riding a bicycle. P.S.F.B. Page 50.
Mark Twain with Helen. N.Y.P.L. Page 50.
At the typewriter. L.C. Page 51.
Letter from Helen to Mr. Gilman. P.S.F.B. Pages 52 and 53.

ACKNOWLEDGMENTS

Our grateful acknowledgment for the full cooperation and kindness and patience of Dr. Edward Waterhouse, Miller Cook, Marilyn S. Kuiper, and Florence J. Worth of the Perkins School for the Blind in Watertown, Massachusetts. Our equal gratitude to the American Foundation for the Blind—its executive director, Dr. M. Robert Barnett; the head of the Department of Public Education, Elisabeth Olesen Garvais; and librarian Helga Lende.

Our deep thanks, too, to the Volta Bureau in Washington, Central Institute for the Deaf in St. Louis, the Long Island Hearing and Speech Society and Jean W. Leigh.

We also wish to thank Mason Tolman of the New York State Library, Albany, New York. Our appreciation, as always, to Romana Javitz, head of the Picture Collection of the New York Public Library and her staff of picture librarians: Louise Leak, Franziska Gay Schacht, Marion Wiethorn, and Polly Magrish. We also thank the staff of the Picture Department of the Library of Congress and the National Archives in Washington, D.C.

For J. J. Fletcher, Herbert Starlight, Peter Sansone, James Hernandez, Marty Monroe, Mae Fargo, Philip H. Miller, Robert Mitchell, Jack Simon, Harry Connors, Otto L. Bettmann, D. Jay Culver, Marston Hamlin, Elma Masut, Shirley Baig our added thanks for their extra kindness.

And for Shirley Green, Richard Craven, Aileen Harrity, Marjorie Martin, Evelyn Sharpe, Irene Anastos, Robert and Pearl Nisenson, Dick Hanley, our personal appreciation for all their assistance.

189